THE LONG LOST BOOKS
OF RAMPA

FEATURING – *MY VISIT TO AGHARTA*

T. Lobsang Rampa

INNER LIGHT PUBLICATIONS

THE LONG LOST BOOKS OF
T. LOBSANG RAMPA, FEATURING. . .
MY VISIT TO AGHARTA

ISBN 1892062348
**Timothy Green Beckley, Editorial Director ● Art & Editorial Consultant, Carol Ann Rodriuez
Covers and graphics by Tim Swartz**

CONTENTS

My Visit To Agharta

JUST WHO WAS T. LOBSANG RAMPA?

The mystery of T. Lobsang Rampa started with the release of his first book *The Third Eye* in 1956. This book, an autobiographical tale of Rampa's study and mastery of Tibetan Buddhism, galvanized the Western world and started a stampede of interest in the Eastern mysteries.

However, with the success of *The Third Eye*, there were those who sought their own publicity by undertaking an investigation on the identity of Tuesday Lobsang Rampa. A group of Tibetan scholars in Britain hired a detective, Clifford Burgess, to look into Rampa's claims. Burgess discovered that Rampa was Cyril Henry Hoskins, who had been born in Devon, England.

Rampa/Hoskins was not deterred by the petty jealousies of his detractors – instead, he revealed that Lobsang Rampa was a *Walk-In* who, with the agreement of Hoskins, took over the Englishman's body in 1949 in order to fulfill his mission on Earth. That mission was to teach the Eastern mysteries to a Western world that had lost touch with their true spiritual nature. Rampa would continue to write about his former life in Tibet, as well as teaching about ancient wisdom's and reawakening our own psychic abilities, up until his physical death in 1981.

Out of his twelve published books, Rampa's most controversial was *My Visit to Venus* (now published by **Inner Light Publications**). *My Visit to Venus* detailed Rampa's amazing contacts with superior beings from other planets and was originally intended for an earlier book, but was removed at the last minute when the publisher decided the public was not ready for such incredible UFO disclosures. Rampa had intended to release other books after *My Visit to Venus*, but due to the negative reaction and criticism he received, he decided that mankind was indeed not yet ready for these revelations. How this book, *My Visit to Agharta*, was finally discovered is a fascinating story.

Back in the 1950's a man named Jim Rigberg ran the **Flying Saucer News Bookstore** located in Spanish Harlem in New York City. Rigberg had befriended Rampa, being the only publisher who paid him (albeit a very small amount) to reprint *My Visit to Venus* in newspaper format (it was a four-page foldout). As a courtesy, Rampa from time to time sent Jim envelopes of his rejected writings – one of these envelopes, discovered among Rigberg's possessions, contained this story by Rampa detailing his journey to the Hollow Earth. Now for the first time ever, **Inner Light Publications** is proud to bring you an incredible story by one of the most intriguing writers of our time – T. Lobsang Rampa.

Timothy Green Beckley

My Visit To Agharta

THE LONG LOST BOOKS OF RAMPA
Section One
My Visit To Agharta

At one time in my life, when I was very young, I had imagined all the wonderful things in the universe and the mysteries contained within its ethereal boundaries. I pondered if I would ever have the chance to experience anything fantastic and different from the prosaic world of my childhood. Now, with the experience of decades, I can look back on my life since those far-off childhood days, and wonder anew what amazing things still lie ahead of me waiting to carry my soul across time and space to reveal the infinite mysteries of creation.

There is so much that I will never know. Perhaps it is our eternal fate to struggle for the unknowable, to seek knowledge that is unattainable in its ultimate infinity. The small grains of information that we are able to grasp are but a tiny part of a beach that stretches on forever, maddening in its vastness, yet compelling in its ultimate riches.

My teachers have shown me the majestic wonders of our own planet and the mind-boggling splendors of the celestial worlds (See: *My Visit To Venus*, Inner Light Publications). I scarcely dreamed that after the privileges my humble soul was allowed in the past that I would be once again offered a journey with my guides to partake of what may be the ultimate destination of Earths ascended masters. A journey that would take me to the ancient and unknown worlds beneath our feet and on to great Agharta.

It had been many months since my journey beyond Earth in the outer space crafts that are called "flying saucers" by the press. I had been told by my guide that my body must "reacclimate" itself to the earth plane before I could take any further sojourns. I had no idea at the time what he meant by that cryptic statement – so I was left to use my imagination on what lay ahead.

To understand the intricate connections that exist in our reality it should be remembered that we are creatures of the Spirit. We are like electric charges endowed with intelligence. Life consists of rapidly vibrating matter generating an electrical charge, the electricity is the Life of Matter. Our bodies are charged with energy that resonates at the level of our existence. In order to physically travel to other worlds and realities, we must be able to change our bodies' electrical resonance to match the location we are travelling. When we return to our own time and space, we must allow our energies the chance to stabilize before we attempt further explorations.

When we are in the physical world we tend to think that only the physical world matters. That is one of the safety devices of the Overself; if we remembered the spirit world with its happiness we would be able to remain here only by a strong effort of will. If we remembered past lives when, perhaps, we were more important than in this life, we should not have the necessary humility.

The time finally came one night as I lay trying to sleep. My conscious mind slowly relented and allowed my astral self to leave its material shell to seek whatever comforts were available in the astral worlds. Scarcely had I left my body when I was overwhelmed by the feeling of warmth and incredible love. Appearing before me was my beloved Guide and friend, the Lama Mingyar Dondup.

Unlike some, It did not surprise me to see my friend in this environment. I knew that the Lama Mingyar Dondup had toured the world, both in the physical and the astral. However, it had been so long since our last adventure that I was genuinely surprised and overjoyed at our unexpected meeting.

"My good friend," I said to him. "It has been way too long since we last spoke."

The Lama laughed a rich and vibrant laugh, full of energy and vitality. The Master was ancient by our standards, yet here he was young and healthy. His happiness and vigor was clearly evident in his brightly shining aura.

"Lobsang," he finally spoke. "It has been but a blink of the eye since our last meeting. You forget that you have been vibrationally tuned to the Earth plane and subject to the illusion of time."

He was right of course. Living in the material world, we are caught up in the artificial concepts of time – the sun rising and setting – the progression of the seasons. Yet, without these abstract concepts to maintain order and assure survival of the physical, our minds would be overwhelmed and driven to madness. Our physical brains act somewhat like a check valve to reality; allowing in only what is really needed for everyday survival. A large part of my training by the Lamas of Tibet has consisted of learning to bypass the brain to get a clearer view of reality.

"You have seen much Lobsang!" said my Guide. "But much has remained hidden from you. Now is the time for you to once again journey with me to see the wonders of our universe. You are ready to see that which only a chosen few has ever been allowed. This is a great responsibility, and is not to be taken lightly. Few have been allowed the opportunity that awaits you."

"Sir!" I replied. "You once told me that the man who sets out upon one of life's paths, falters, and turns back, is no man. I will go ahead in spite of knowing the difficulties before me."

He smiled, and nodded his approval.

"As I expected," he said. "Your curiosity has taken you to many great places, you will always succeed in the end."

As always with our adventures, I was keen to begin straight away.

"I am ready to leave with you now," I said.

Once again I could sense the amusement and joy emanating from the being of white light before me. His affection and love for me sparkled across the very essence of his astral being.

"This will be a journey that you will take in your physical body dear friend," he said. "You have one week to prepare. Be outside your house at this time in seven days. We will come to take you then. You will be gone for seven days, so make the proper arrangements for what you leave behind."

Before I could further question my friend, he withdrew from me and I found myself once again in the physical. I had seven days to wonder what adventure lay before me. But I had no time to worry, if I was to be gone for a week, I had to make immediate preparations to cover for my absence.

My Visit To Agharta

A STRANGE CRAFT BECKONS

The week went quickly by as I made ready my leave. I arranged for a good friend, who understood the necessity of my frequent trips, to stay over and watch my house. Her most important task of course would be to watch over my beautiful cats, who never understood why in my travels I should dare leave them behind. But finally I was ready and spent the remaining time in quiet prayer and meditation.

As I stood in the quiet dark of my garden, the March air still crisp with a frozen reminder of winter, I looked out over the sleeping countryside and pondered the night sky ablaze with its infinite stars.

I had seen and discovered so much in my amazing life that it scarcely seemed possible, concerning my very humble beginnings, that my life wasn't just some incredible and wonderful dream and I would at any moment awaken to find myself back in the horrors that was me and my life so long ago.

I was a sorrowful man who in my darkest moment could very well have snuffed out the candle of life that was not mine to take. But instead of being swallowed up by infinity and immediately reborn to start again, I was instead joined in both body and spirit by the essence and being of Lobsang Rampa.

We became one and we understood our mission and purpose in this lifetime. Where there was once only despair, there was now knowledge, hope and purpose. It was because of this that I now stood alone in the night, silently awaiting the magnificence that was now my life.

One star in particular stood out in the velvet firmament. It twinkled wildly with an iridescent rainbow of colour that drew my attention to it immediately. It seemed to slowly grow in size as it whirled on its vertical axis like a glowing ball of nebulous light. I knew from past experience that this was the light ship I had been told to await.

Anyone else who may have observed this amazing phenomena would be correct in saying that he saw a UFO. For me, however, there was nothing unidentified about this craft, I knew it was a vehicle constructed of energy by the combined mental powers of enlightened beings.

My Visit To Agharta

Even before my own experiences with the flying saucers, I was curious about the true nature of UFOs and the exciting possibilities that we were being visited by beings from other planets. I had been told by some of the other Lamas that certain UFOs were the ancient air vehicles flown by men who had fled the surface world to live in the caverns underground. At the time I found this incredible because I could not imagine why anyone would want to live in such dark, damp surroundings. Nevertheless, I was assured that many places beneath our feet were beautiful, healthy places to live and prosper.

I would later learn that our humble world is constantly being visited by craft from not only other worlds and planets in the universe, but from other dimensions, realities and times. The entire universe is awash with life and intelligent beings, and planet Earth, like other inhabited worlds, is always a place of interest for these fantastic creatures. Someday, mankind as well will travel the universe in the very same ships of light and energy, visiting other worlds and times in our never-ending quest for knowledge and enlightenment. This will be a time of great joy and happiness for all.

As I continued to watch, the "star" began to slowly move back and forth in the sky, not unlike a pocket watch dangling at the end of its chain. At the same time it began to grow larger and brighter, no doubt an illusion caused by its rapid approach straight for me.

The night was quiet in an unearthly manner. It was as if I were the only living creature on the planet. I felt isolated not only from physical reality, but also on an astral level. I had noticed the same effect when we first came into close contact with the other worldly aircraft in the Hidden Valley. But here, in my own garden, the effect held a wholly new sensation for me.

I was torn by my feelings of awe and fear. One part of me wanted to go with the light, to become one forever with it. While another, more primitive side of me, wanted to scream in terror and flee as fast as I could. Even though my more enlightened self knew that no harm could come to me, my deepest, oldest instincts still managed to send a deep shudder throughout my entire being.

Slowly the light began to descend. Its movements made it appear as if it were a leaf falling from a tree in autumn. At the same time its colour started to shift from

My Visit To Agharta

a blazing white light to shades of red, orange and violet. I cannot describe the utter beauty of the colours that were being emitted from the strange device.

It was if I were seeing these colours for the first time in my life. Never before, nor since, have I seen such incredible colours either manmade or in nature. It is something I will never forget.

It was apparent to me that I was seeing energy shifting and slowing its vibrational field to coalesce into solid matter. The incredible power that must be required for such a monumental task left me wondering if my simple human mind could ever grasp the concept behind it. Yet there was no denying that such a feat was possible as I was seeing it with my own eyes. The colours continued to brighten and shift as the object changed shape.

Looking now like a brightly coloured soap bubble, the craft settled down not more than twenty metres ahead and floated just above the ground. Seeming to radiate from within, the opalescent glow disappeared and I could now see that the ship was disc-shaped, like two Tibetan bowls placed rim to rim. The surface was a dull grey, somewhat like pewter. Occasionally a pulsation of some kind would ripple across its surface giving it a liquid metal look, somewhat like solidified mercury.

I could not resist the stray thought that perhaps I was looking at something that went far beyond what we would call metal or plastic. The feeling that emanated from the craft like heat waves on a summer day, bore the distinct impression of consciousness and even intelligence. The ship was not only alive, it had a mind. I could feel its thoughts irradiating me as it probed my very being with its consciousness. For the briefest of moments I became one with this magnificent intelligence and understood its creation and purpose. But, just as quickly, it withdrew from my mind and I was once again alone.

Obviously satisfied that it had found the person it had been sent for, a door appeared on the lower section of the craft. The door seemed to grow foggy and transparent and then disappeared completely leaving a rectangle of white light that seemed to beckon me forward. How could I resist such a blatant invitation? Even if I had not been expecting something like this, I am sure that I would have succumbed to my natural curiosity and gone inside.

My Visit To Agharta

Stepping through the door I experienced what seemed to be a slight electric shock as I crossed the threshold. There was apparently an energy field of some kind inside the craft. I could only suppose its purpose was to keep separate the outside environment from the inside. But now I felt no further ill effects.

Once inside I had expected to be greeted by the same superior beings from other worlds that had taken us on our previous travels beyond Earth. But instead of the Tall One or the Broad One, the interior of the ship was empty. I could see no controls or machinery of any kind. Instead, a white light that had no apparent source filled my surroundings to such a degree that I could see nothing else. It was as if I were inside a flourescent tube, with the exception that this light was not bright and harsh, but pleasurable and relaxing.

"I am honored by your presence Lobsang Rampa," a pleasant voice suddenly spoke out.

"I am the one who is honored," I replied while bowing to the invisible voice. "It is a great privilege to be with you on this fantastic ship, but won't you appear to me?"

"Thank you my friend," replied the voice. "But you can already see me, for I am all around you. I am your host and mode of transport this evening."

The words made perfect sense. The feelings I had outside that I was in the presence of a living being were very correct. This was not simply a mechanical contrivance of some kind, a wonderful machine built of exotic metals and plastics, but a fantastic living creature beyond any sort that I had ever imagined.

"If it is not an improper question, might I enquire what sort of being you might be?" I asked hesitantly.

"It is not improper at all," said the voice. "It is with questions that we learn and grow. I am happy to answer to the best of my abilities any questions that you might have."

"Splendid," I said happily. "I have never seen anything such as yourself. Are you an artificial intelligence like a robot?"

My Visit To Agharta

"No, I am a living being much as yourself," explained the voice.

"Could you explain?" I asked.

"As you are well aware," the voice said. "The principal essence of our universe and the infinite number of other universes is consciousness. Our reality could not exist without consciousness. This living essence prevails throughout the known realities. Its source is the unknown outside the material and astral worlds. You, your fellow humans, myself and countless other life forms throughout all universes are part of this consciousness. It is infinite and we are all one with it.

"Those such as myself are beings of pure energy. We exist throughout all known realities. We are not constrained by time and space for we exist in the realms beyond and within the material world. We are often used by other species as a mode of transport. This is because we are not constrained by time and space. Creation in its entirety is within our reach."

The voice I noticed seemed to be neither male or female in its tone and inflections. Instead it seemed a perfect and harmonious combination of the two, speaking with a melodious cadence that was both pleasant and soothing to hear.

"I have heard of beings such as you," I said to my unseen host. "You have been called many names throughout the ages. My brothers from Tibet call you 'Tulpas' and western magickal writings refer to you as 'elementals.'

"Those are merely names in an attempt to understand that which cannot be understood," the ship replied. "It is true that we have known humans since the beginning of time. But we also know the other races throughout creation, for we are everywhere and part of everything. You will learn someday that all living creatures can be just as free as we are.

"Because of our ability to change our vibrational rate, we can temporarily become solid in the material worlds. When we are seen by living creatures we can be molded by impressions in the viewers mind and often we are seen as strange creatures such as the Yeti, aliens, or even deities. We have been blamed for much over the centuries, but it is actually your minds that have given us form and had us play your roles based on your belief systems."

My Visit To Agharta

My Visit To Agharta

"Fantastic," I thought. There was so much about the nature of our world that I yearned to know that I could have stood and talked to my new friend for hours. Unfortunately my travelling companion announced that our journey was already at an end.

"You have someone here who is anxious to see you," the ship said. "We will meet again, so don't despair. We will talk again soon, I promise."

This came as a great surprise to me because I had sensed no movement of the ship to indicate that we were anywhere but the garden behind my home. Nevertheless, the open door showed that we had indeed travelled far from my backyard garden.

Stepping outside the cold air struck me immediately. I could see through the pre-dawn mist that I was now high in the mountains somewhere. The towering peaks were unfamiliar and rose almost vertically from my vantage point. The gray, craggy rocks were totally devoid of any plant life and seemed menacing and hostile to interlopers such as myself.

AN OLD FRIEND

On a lonely outcropping of rock scarcely large enough to contain us, the ship had precariously landed and now seemed to attach itself to the mountain, turning the same rocky, gray colour as its surroundings. I could no longer tell if it was simply hiding itself or if it had disappeared completely. I was now all alone.

All around me was nothing but rock so bare and utterly without colour or life that I could have been on the moon instead of somewhere on Earth. Beside me, stretching off into the distance, was a mountain range of immense size and splendor. I was certain that few men had ever gazed upon this unknown land.

Against the face of the mountain was a fissure that in some ancient time had cracked open the living rock and formed a natural grotto. Just inside this shelter I could see the flickering glow of a small fire and smell the sweet smoke of burning wood. Since there was no one outside on the ledge to greet me, I decided that my place was to be in front of the fire, rather than shivering outside in the hostile elements.

My Visit To Agharta

Inside, the cave was pleasantly warm and smokey. A distinctly friendlier environment than the cold, uninviting mountains outside. Seated in front of the fire with his back to me sat a man clad in the traditional robes of a Tibetan Lama. I recognized instantly my friend of many years, whose astral invitation had brought me to this strange, wild land, the Lama Mingyar Dondup.

"Master," I said, bowing deeply with my hands clasped together in the typical Tibetan greeting. "I have come as you requested."

"Welcome Lobsang," he replied without turning his head. "Come warm yourself in front of the fire."

I seated myself cross-legged on the ground opposite my Guide. The fire between us cast a flickering light upon his face. I had known Mingyar Dondup for many years, yet his face still appeared as strong and youthful as when we first met.

"Have some tea," he said, motioning towards the pot near the fire. "It is my one weakness. You know I never travel without it."

This was very true. Many of our sessions together over the years were accompanied by cups of Indian tea, a rich tea perfect for the cold, bleak weather of the Himalayas. Compared to the bland, mass produced teas found in England, this tea was thick with flavor, with a character as complex and unique as the far-away lands in which it was produced.

Sipping my tea, I motioned to the rocky walls around us and asked: "Master, could you tell me where we are? I don't recognize the mountains around us. It is all so unfamiliar."

"These mountains are far to the north of our own Himalayas," he told me. "They are part of the Tian Shan mountain range. But you will not find this particular range on any map. It is almost unexplored due to its nearly unscalable cliffs. We are now deep in a part of Asia that not only is inaccessible by the hazards of the landscape, but also by the local governments and current political situation. This area is forbidden territory as it is said the nearby Pamir plateau was once the garden of Eden. I doubt that many men outside the area know that these mountains even exist."

My Visit To Agharta

My Guide's words sent a thrilling shiver down my back. As a young man I had often dreamed of travelling abroad and being the first to explore strange places and unknown lands. Now, here I was sitting in a cave on an little-known range of mountains in a land not familiar with the feet of man. I was frightfully awed by what was happening, and deeply honored at the same time.

We sat in front of the fire talking for hours. We reminisced about our past adventures and the friends we knew. Finally, fatigue overcame me and I placed my mat back from the fire so not to be singed from the occasional flying ember. As I fell asleep, I could see my friend and Guide, still seated in front of the fire, his eyes closed in silent prayer.

It seemed that I had scarcely closed my eyes when I was awakened by the smell of freshly brewed tea. Beside me was a small cup of hot tea and several small cakes. The Master, who appeared not to have moved from his spot in front of the fire, was finishing his own breakfast.

"It is time that we begin our journey," the Master said as he arose and began gathering his belongings. "We have far to go before we can rest, and I'm afraid where we bed next will not be in as comfortable of surroundings as we enjoy now."

Quickly finishing my tea and cakes, I picked up my backpack and buckled it around my shoulders. It wasn't particularly heavy as years of experience had taught me to travel as light as possible. Mingyar Dondups pack was even smaller than my own. No doubt made up of a simple mat, a blanket, and the provisions for preparing tea.

Following my Guide, we walked to the back of the cave where the light of the fire grew dim. The wall seemed no different than the rest of the cave, but the Lama evidently knew that this section was special as he reached out and pushed hard against the rocks.

Slowly, a boulder that had been deliberately set and balanced to such a fine degree that with a little effort it could be swivelled to the side, moved and revealed a hidden opening. Motioning me to follow, my Guide stepped past the rocky portal and into the hidden passage. After we entered, the rock slid back into place and we were plunged into darkness.

My Visit To Agharta

"Master!" I exclaimed in panic.

"Quiet," came his stern reply from the blackness. "Have patience."

The darkness enveloped us to such a degree that I thought I had been struck down and removed of all my senses. Neither light or sound could penetrate this black. It was a darkness devoid of any form or substance.

The Masters voice suddenly spoke out: "Look," he said. "There is a light!"

I strained my eyes, but the darkness remained unchanged.

"I see nothing," I said.

But I realized that I was starting to see shapes and forms. The darkness was slowly being replaced by a strange glow. The light was a beautiful range of subtle colors that reminded me of a warm summer day with a sky so blue you could lose yourself in it forever. I looked upwards, expecting to see an opening to the outside, but there seemed no direct source for this wonderful light. It was as if the air itself was luminous.

"It is so beautiful," I exclaimed in wonder. "Where does it come from?"

"This is the technology of men who lived on the Earth long before the creatures that would become humans had even crawled from the sea," was his reply.

I understood the words, but the meaning still evaded me.

"But how can this be," I wondered out loud. "There were no men on Earth before us. Only simple life in the ancient seas. It is impossible."

"Not so Lobsang," said the Lama. "The Earth is incredibly old. It is far older than scientists believe. What we were taught as the time of birth of our planet was simply the most recent wave of life to sweep it. There have been countless other waves as there will be countless more. We are not the first, nor will we be the last."

The Lama turned from me and started to walk down the passageway.

My Visit To Agharta

"We had better continue," he said.

The passageway that we were now in was roughly circular in shape and wide enough for ten men walking abreast to travel comfortably. The floors, walls and ceiling were of solid rock that had an odd, glassy texture. But unlike glass, the floor was not slick and very easy on the feet. I could conjecture that this tunnel had been somehow melted into shape. Perhaps with a high-energy device similar to a laser beam.

Silently the two of us continued on through the featureless tunnel. I could tell that it was slowly leading us downwards into the very heart of the mountains.

"No one knows who really built this passage through the rock," Mingyar Dondup suddenly spoke up. "It was made so long ago that nothing remains of that civilisation. They have utterly vanished into the dust of countless ages. Not even a name exists to those that walked on this planet during its infant days."

"But this tunnel was made with modern techniques Master," I replied rubbing the smooth wall. "No one could have made this except in the last few years."

I had heard stories of secret underground fortresses built by governments and the military. Some were made as bomb shelters, others as secret bases of operation. This tunnel must obviously lead to such a facility, either built by the Communist Chinese, or even more daring, the Soviet Union or the United States. It appeared too shiny and new to be anything else other than another folly made by aggressive and paranoid humans.

"No human technology built this tunnel my friend," the Lama laughed. "This tunnel and thousands like it all over the world were here and already ancient when men first strode out of Africa. In fact, this particular passageway was here long before the mountains above. It is made of a substance that can stretch and mold itself as the earth shifts and folds from tectonic pressures."

"Where does it lead?" I asked.

"This tunnel is the beginning of a long journey that will take us into the very heart of our world," answered the Lama. "We are privileged to be allowed to see

18

the secret and hidden lands at the center of the planet. We are going to beloved Agharta."

Agharta. The very name struck me with a force that took my breath away. This was the subterranean kingdom at the Earth's center where the king of the world reigned and no living man could ever look upon. I had heard the name a thousand times, but I scarcely believed that such a place truly existed. It was as if a Christian had been told that he could walk around the block and visit Heaven. It was that unbelievable.

Ancient writings called the Puranas speak of the underground world. One such Puranic comment has to do with the narration of the Kalki avatar: at the end of Kali Yuga, the Kalki Avatar will be born in the best of Brahmin families of the city of Shambala to annihilate miscreants on the surface of the globe. Afterwards, the general Puranic version goes, men will come to the surface from the interior of the planet to recolonize and re-start Vedic culture. It is noteworthy that Shamballa is mentioned in the Puranas as a city of the planet's interior. Not only in the Puranas, but also in the Tibetan collective memory, Shambala is deemed to be a city in the Earth's interior.

There is another prominent Puranic story which openly makes reference to the hollow portion of the Earth. It is the story of the sons of Maharaj Sagara. Indra had stolen the sacrificial horse meant for the ashvamedha sacrifice (a type of fire sacrifice). As the story goes, his sons went searching after the horse and came to a Northern ocean, which they travelled over, and entered into the "bowels" of the Earth. There, they found the horse at the hermitage of Kapila Rishi. The sons of Sagara manhandled the Rishi even though he swore that it wasn't he who had stolen the horse.

Few societies exist that did not have some kind of myth or legend of the underground world and the people who dwelled within. One of the main tenants of the Mesopotamian, Egyptian, Greek and American Indian myths of creation is that man was created in the underworld, and then was sent or migrated to the surface.

In the Greek myths, man was thus created from clay and fire in the womb of the goddess Gaea, who personified Mother Earth. Similarly, in the older Mesopotamian myths, man was created in the womb of Mami or Ninharsag, (Lady of the

Mountain) who likewise personified the Earth. We know of this today as the sacred Garden of Eden, or the Isle of the Blessed.

Louis Pauwels and Jacques Bergier in their book **The Morning of the Magicians**, wrote: "This idea of a Hollow Earth is connected with a tradition which is to be found everywhere throughout the ages. The most ancient religious texts speak of a separate world situated underneath the Earth's crust which was supposed to be the dwelling-place of departed spirits. When Gilgamesh, the legendary hero of the ancient Sumerian and Babylonian epics, went to visit his ancestor Utnapishtim, he descended into the bowels of the Earth; and it was there that Orpheus went to seek the soul of Euridice. Ulysses, having reached the furthermost boundaries of the Western world, offered a sacrifice so that the spirits of the Ancients would rise up from the depths of the Earth and give him advice. Pluto was said to reign over the underworld and over the spirits of the dead. The souls of the damned went to live in caverns beneath the Earth."

THE SECRET CAVERNS

We continued down the unchanging tunnel as Mingyar Dondup regaled me with ancient adventures of brave and noble humans who, either by purpose or accident, travelled to the underworld and returned. He told of gods and demigods who guarded their forbidden cities from any and all outsiders. To cross one of these mystical beings meant certain death for all mortal interlopers.

It had seemed we had journeyed for hours. Neither the passageway nor the light changed. We could have travelled for hundreds of kilometres or a few steps, the tunnel was unchanging.

Due to the nature of the light and purity of the atmosphere, we could see for quite a distance either ahead or behind us. Only the slight downward curve of the tunnel interfered with how far we could see. After awhile, It became apparent to me that I could see a change of colour in the tunnel before us. And as we grew closer I could clearly see that we were approaching a section of the tunnel that had been intersected by another.

Because of our long hours in a perfectly unchanging environment, the excitement I now felt was almost unbearable. My eyes had been aching for even the slightest bit of change in colour or difference in texture. But now my senses were overwhelmed by the sheer size of the opening and chaotic appearance of the tunnel walls. Whoever was responsible for this intrusion had used methods to breach the rock completely dissimilar from the original builders.

"Ah, here is our first stop," the Master said happily. "We can rest here for awhile."

On opposite sides of the tunnel were great holes that looked as if they had been blasted through with a massive force. I could see that the offending tunnel was crudely constructed with none of the finesse of the original. The new passageway, like the other, also stretched off into the distance. Despite its crude nature, I could only marvel at what efforts were required to dig such fantastic passageways through the planet's crust. Mankind had barely scratched the surface compared to these marvelous constructions.

"This is as far as we can go alone," the Lama said to me. "To go any further by ourselves would be foolhardy and dangerous. We must now rest here and wait. We will be joined soon by someone more familiar with these caves and their possible hazards."

A fire in these surroundings seemed out of the question. It wasn't needed for warmth, as the tunnel maintained a constant temperature comfortable to its travelers. And it wasn't needed for its light, as the passageways illumination never wavered in its intensity. Nevertheless, fire was needed for the brewing of tea. And to not have hot tea after such a long journey was almost certainly uncivilized.

However, before I could broach the question, the Lama collected the tea pot filled with water and placed it against the wall of the glassy tunnel. A few seconds later he brought it back and filled our cups with what was now hot water. I could not understand how this could happen.

Earlier, I had touched the walls with my bare hands finding them cool to the skin. But now, a pot filled with cold water was heated to nearly boiling in just a few seconds. It was as if the tunnel knew what was needed and it responded in kind. This was a science beyond anything ever taught to me in school. I would soon learn that such marvels were commonplace here in the underground world.

My Visit To Agharta

We drank our tea and ate what small provisions we brought with us. The Master spoke of the dangers of travelling the caves.

"There are men who live close to the surface world," he said. "Some were part of a race that went underground before the last ice age. Others have been down here longer. They couldn't take their "science" with them, so they were forced to live in primitive conditions. Many of their descendants have degenerated into inhuman beasts who hunt each other, and sometimes surface people, for food and sport. They are despicable creatures who exist only for the pleasures of the flesh. They have lost their humanity and their souls."

"They sound like the demons of legend," I speculated. "They lived deep underground and came to the surface to bedevil and plague all humans and mock the Creator at every opportunity."

"Even legends have their beginnings, Lobsang," agreed my friend. "But I'm sure you must be tired after our pleasant walk, you should sleep now as tomorrow will take us even further into the inner recesses of the world."

"Pleasant walk, indeed," I thought as I unpacked my mat. This was the Masters idea of a fine joke. I felt as if we had already walked halfway to the center of the Earth. It certainly hadn't been a restful stroll through the garden.

The Master in turn was unrolling his mat for sleep, so despite my reservations about rest in this strange place, I too settled down and soon surrendered to sweet slumber.

A STRANGE DREAM

Perhaps it was the strange surrounding, or the unwelcome intrusion of thousands of probing, curious minds, but my sleep was invaded by unsettling dreams of a strange nature. In my dreams I was one with some kind of creature who lived in this underworld. I had only the slightest of intelligence and awareness of who I was and of those around me. My emotions were like that of a child – manic, untethered, wild, soaring to the extremes of happiness and anger. I was also filled with hunger that was unending and all-consuming. It filled my mind and soul almost to the brink of madness.

My Visit To Agharta

I dreamt that I was hunting with my family. We were a small group made up of mothers, fathers, aunts, uncles, cousins, brothers and sisters. We sometimes joined up with others to hunt, but like all of our kind, we kept mostly to ourselves.

Our kind were relative newcomers to the caves. Even if my host wasn't aware of it, my human mind knew that these creatures were at one time humans who entered the caves thousands of years ago. We had given up civilisation and reverted back to the animal state of our primitive beginnings. And why not? What did civilisation give to us except disaster, misery and the near destruction of our kind? We had no choice but to go underground and survive. And if survival meant throwing off the fakery of civilisation and society, then so be it.

We weren't the only ones here though. The tunnels and caverns were filled with millions of beings, some primitive and wild like us, others were intelligent and technologically oriented.

Over the millenniums we have adapted to our new environment. To keep out the cold, our hair is now long and covers the entire body. Our nails are long and sharp, as are our teeth. We are smaller, faster, and more crafty than our sick, corrupted forefathers when they first came to the caves. We are survivors.

I realize that we are slowly surrounding our unsuspecting prey. We silently take our positions so that there can be no escape. From my hiding spot I can now see our quarry. It is a young male from one of the more developed groups. He is hairless and is wearing manufactured clothes. It has been a long time since we hunted in these tunnels. The inhabitants have lost their fear of travelling alone and have grown unwary. It makes hunting that much easier for us. And why shouldn't it be easy for us? We have to eat and we serve a purpose to the creator like all living things. It is our purpose to hunt those who are weak or lame. We maintain the balance of nature.

With loud screams, the women and young ones dash from the rocks towards their startled prey. The human, who appears no older than fourteen years, leaps from his resting spot and tries to escape. Little does he realize that the shouting mass of woman and children are cleverly driving him into the waiting clutches of the adult males who are hidden around a bend in the tunnel. I am amongst this group that eagerly await our prey.

My Visit To Agharta

Before the young man even has a chance to shout, the adult males swarm over the doomed youth and drag him to the ground, their teeth ripping at his throat and tearing the tender flesh. I join the adults and savage his abdomen with my nails in an attempt to disembowel him. There is no escaping his fate, and the young human finally dies when his neck is broken and throat torn out.

There is no formality, we eat our prey on the spot. The larger males get the first, sweet blood that pours from the young man's neck. The rest of us tear at his flesh, ripping huge chunks that we greedily shove into our mouths and devour. When we finish, there will be little remaining save a few splashes of blood to show that the young man even once existed.

For awhile there will be a few more easy victims in this area. Then the rest will grow cautious and we will have to move on. But time is our friend and they will grow complacent once more and we will be back. They always forget and we always return.

I awoke with a start, the dream still fresh on my mind. I could still taste the salty tang of blood, and feel the still quivering flesh between my teeth. I looked at my hands, half expecting them to still be covered in the gore of the murdered young man. My physical hands were clean, but my soul felt tainted and blackened by the imposing dream.

Had it been real? Had I actually shared the body of some half-human creature that lived deep underground and preyed on other people? Or was it just some fantastic dream delved from some deep, forgotten place in my mind? I shuddered to think that my own subconscious could ever come up with such horrifying images. So I concluded that the experience had been very real. I had somehow tuned into the mind of a savage creature that lived nearby. I now knew for certain that the tunnels were indeed dangerous. Travel from now on must be conducted with an extra degree of caution lest we are taken by surprise by the same creatures whose breakfast I had just shared. I did not savor such a reunion anytime soon.

I gathered up my mat and looked around for the Master. I spotted him seated cross-legged by the junction of tunnels. He was not alone.

Seeing that I was awake, he motioned me to approach.

My Visit To Agharta

"Ah, I am glad to see that you decided to join us on this expedition Lobsang," he joked. "I was afraid that you would sleep away our allotted time."

The stranger, sitting with the Lama, was a man about thirty years old and wearing a light gray shirt and slacks. His skin was unusual, appearing deeply tanned with an underlying olive green colour. His eyes were slightly larger than normal and slanted downwards, giving him an oriental appearance. His cheekbones were high and his chin was sharp and pointed. His mouth was small and surrounded by almost featureless lips. He seemed very human, but with features that I did not recognize on people from the surface world. This was a strange fellow indeed.

"You must try this food our new friend has brought us," said the Master handing me a bowl filled with vegetables.

I gingerly poked at the contents of the bowl with my chop sticks. Some of the ingredients looked like chunks of meat. I maintained a vegetarian diet, but especially after my disturbing dream I did not fancy eating any kind of meat at the moment.

The stranger, watching me inspect my breakfast, laughed a deep laugh and said: "You don't have to worry Bub. It only looks like meat. I know cooks who can take mushrooms and soy beans and make dishes that you would swear to your gods were made with real meat, so go on and enjoy."

True to his word, the meal was excellent and filling. We washed it down with cups of hot Indian tea. As we shared some sweet cakes I got to know our visitor.

"Leo's what you can call me," he said. "I'm not going to tell you my real name because that is only known to my family. Its bad luck to let outsiders know your true name you know."

"Our new friend will be our escort from now on," the Master said. "His people are known throughout the planet as excellent guides to the tunnels. We wouldn't dare go any further without their help."

"Are you from the surface world?" I asked. "I don't think I have ever seen anyone quite like yourself."

My Visit To Agharta

Leo laughed at my question.

"Oh no," he said. "I come from a town beneath the surface. Our people have lived below ground for a very long time. Unlike others who moved into the caves, we maintained contact with the surface world. For a price, we do 'favors' for those on the surface. Sometimes things need to be done that only we can do – things that can't be trusted to a surface dweller.

"There are powerful people in your world who know all about the peoples that live beneath their feet. We've done their dirty work since the beginning of your civilisation. That is if the price is right."

"You're a 'hired gun?'"I asked, somewhat taken aback by his candor.

"You could put it that way Bub," he answered. "We're businessmen. We work for a living. We bring down much needed supplies to our people in exchange for our favors. We play a very important role in the exchange of goods and services from your world to ours. But don't worry. I have been amply paid for my services as your guide on this trip. We are very loyal to our customers."

"Leo has come very highly recommended Lobsang," the Master interjected. "There is no need for mistrust and suspicion."

Though I didn't know it at the time. I later learned that there is a long history in myths and legends of beings very much like our friend Leo. The American Indians called them "Tricksters," supernatural creatures that lived in caves and confounded the Indians with their mischievous, and often deadly games. Certain areas were considered taboo because of the Tricksters.

These beings have also apparently managed to infuse themselves in the flying saucer and conspiracy cultures of the 20th century. The physical descriptions of some UFO occupants and the Men-In-Black, so often reported by flying saucer witnesses and researchers, bear a striking resemblance to the race of people Leo belongs to.

It would seem that there is a conspiracy afoot on the planet that involves certain groups of very powerful and influential people. These people have used their centuries old contacts with the underworld people to create hoaxes and lies concerning flying saucers and the beings flying them.

Possibly these powerful groups are worried that contact with beings from other planets would interfere with their continued world domination. They may have used these underworld "hit men" to frighten or even harm those that may be too close to the "truth." This is pure speculation on my part based on the little bits of information that Leo provided us.

With Leo as our guide, we set off from the glassy tunnel down the new, roughly hewn passageway. Leo explained that these tunnels were dug at a much later date then the glassy tunnels, and were a more direct route to our ultimate destination.

"The glassy tunnels weren't made for foot travel," Leo told us. "They were actually constructed to carry people and supplies from the surface to the cities down below using ancient flying machines called vimanas. We have no idea how old the glass tunnels really are. They were already here when the first of the underground dwellers arrived, so they must be incredibly ancient. Even our legends are at a loss to say how old the tunnels really are."

ANCIENT AIRCRAFT OF THE GODS

For those not familiar with the name, vimanas were highly advanced ancient Indian flying machines mentioned in the great Indian national epic, the Mahabharata. The Mahabharata tells the story of the long war between the Kauravas and the Pandavas. This war was apparently willed by the ancient Indian Gods with the intention of easing the problem of over-population in the world.

It is in the Mahabharata that we hear about Bhima who "flew with his vimana on an enormous ray which was as brilliant as the sun and made a noise like the thunder of a storm." And in the same great ancient Indian epic we also hear about the great warrior Arjuna's ascent to Indra's heaven.

According to legends, Arjuna was not a god, but a mortal. However, during the telling of his particular adventure we are told of his ascent to heaven in a car that travels upwards to the clouds with a noise like thunder. Whilst travelling to heaven Arjuna apparently also sees flying cars that have crashed and are out of action and

27

other flying cars that are stationary, whilst others fly freely in the air. Interestingly in the Mahabharata we also find information about the terrible weapons belonging to the ancient Indian Gods that, in the light of our present day knowledge, do sound eerily like atomic weapons.

In the Ramyana, often cited as the second great Indian epic after the Mahabharata, we are told about vimanas that fly at great heights with the aid of quicksilver and a great propulsive wind. These vimanas could apparently travel vast distances through the air or underground and manoeuver upward, downward and forward. They were magnificent machines fit only for royalty and the gods.

Perhaps the most challenging information about these allegedly mythical vimanas in the ancient records is the precise instructions on how to build one. In the Sanskrit Samarangana Sutradhara, it is written:

"Strong and durable must the body of the vimana be made, like a great flying bird of light material. Inside one must put the mercury engine with its iron heating apparatus underneath. By means of the power latent in the mercury which sets the driving whirlwind in motion, a man sitting inside may travel a great distance in the sky. The movements of the vimana are such that it can vertically ascend, vertically descend, move slanting forwards and backwards. With the help of the machines human beings can fly in the air and heavenly beings can come down to earth."

The Hakatha (Laws of the Babylonians) states quite unambiguously: "The privilege of operating a flying machine is great. The knowledge of flight is among the most ancient of our inheritances. A gift from 'those from upon high'. We received it from them as a means of saving many lives."

More fantastic still is the information given in the ancient Chaldean work, The Sifrala, which contains over one hundred pages of technical details on building a flying machine. It contains words which translate as graphite rod, copper coils, crystal indicator, vibrating spheres, stable angles, and so on.

I marveled at the thought of watching those incredible flying machines shooting up and down the ancient tunnels that connected the inner and surface worlds. Now they were mostly abandoned and unused except for the occasional foot traffic to the hidden exits to the surface. Leo did say that there are sightings once and awhile of strange vehicles that fly up and down the tunnels. Like the flying saucer sightings above ground, the tunnel sightings are mostly considered folklore. Nevertheless, it would not surprise me if the deepest recesses of the planet still hold those who know how to use the ancient technologies of the old ones.

A MOST WONDERFUL LIGHT

As we walked down the tunnel, I again noticed the soft light that seemed to shine from no apparent source. It seemed as if the air itself were luminous, casting a glow over the entire area with a light unlike any on the surface. Perhaps Leo would have a better explanation on where this light came from.

"What is the source of the light?" I asked our guide.

"No one really knows," Leo answered. "Our legends say it was part of the Old Ones' science that has become lost over the millions of years. Others say its astral light created by magic of the Old Ones. Science or magic, is there really any difference?"

"The Old Ones," I said. "I thought your people were the ones who carved these rough tunnels."

"Oh no, it wasn't us," our guide said. "We haven't been down in the caves for that long. No more than 50 or 60 thousand years or so. These and the glass tunnels were already here when we arrived. Of course there are others who have been underground for a lot longer than us, millions of years, and they say the tunnels were here when they were forced to flee to the caves when the sun turned radioactive."

Leo's words may have shocked those who had been taught in school that our society was the only advanced civilisation to have arisen on the planet. I had heard in the past from some of the old Lamas that other powerful civilisations, now lost in time, have risen and fallen on the Earth. But I had never heard of any civilisation as far back as Leo said. Millions of years ago? It was impossible. Yet all through this journey both Leo and my Master have spoken of the incredible age of the caverns and the beings who built them. Still, my mind reeled with questions that needed answers.

My Visit To Agharta

"How could the tunnels be that old?" I asked. People haven't been around that long. Less than a million years I think it is."

"The world's been around for a long time Bub," Leo answered. "She looks pretty good for her age don't you think? Fooled a lot of those snooty scientists on the surface."

"But that doesn't answer. . ." I began, only to be interrupted in mid-question.

"Look – I can't answer your questions friend," Leo said. "All I know is that there have been a lot of people and other things roaming these caverns for a very long time. That's a problem you see. Some of them left their science and machines behind when they left. Those machines were found by some not-so -nice people who like to cause problems, both down here and on the surface. Those machines are so old that no one knows what they were originally built for. Only now they are being used for evil purposes. They have incredible powers that can tear your soul apart. I've seen with my own eyes the damage that these machines can do to a person. There are some incredibly beautiful things down here my friend. But there is also incredible ugliness as well."

The Master, Mingyar Dondup, who had been quietly listening to our conversation, suddenly spoke up.

"We have been taught," he said, "that the creatures who now operate these hateful machines have become sick and twisted, both in body and mind, by their use of the machines. They have grown dependent on the machines radiations – radiations that in times past were used to heal the body and soul. But now the machines are used to hurt and destroy and the radiations sicken and warp those who use them."

Before he could continue, on the path just ahead there appeared a figure wearing a cloak with the hood pulled up to cover its head. The sudden and unexpected appearance made the three of us stop in our tracks in surprise. Despite the fact that the figure was completely covered from head to toe, I could tell that it was a woman under her cloak.

"Err, I didn't smell her coming," Leo said quietly.

My Visit To Agharta

The figure reached up and pulled down the hood to reveal her face. She stared at us with eyes as cold and blue as a Siamese cat.

It shocked me to think that a woman would be out alone in the caves, especially after hearing the tales of savagery and danger from our guide. The caves could be dangerous even for groups of well-armed men. One woman alone was asking for almost certain trouble from the dark denizens that prowl the caves and tunnels.

"Something's not right," Leo hissed.

"I agree," said the Master.

Slowly, her eyes never straying from ours, the woman took off her cloak. At first glance she appeared totally nude. But she was actually wearing a thin, nearly transparent, dress that clung to her body and ended just below her hips.

Her skin was the golden colour of ripened wheat with a hint of olive just below the surface. Her hair, which cascaded down around her shoulders, was silvery with highlights that seemed to sparkle with a life all their own. I could not take my eyes off of her. She seemed to radiate a raw, physical sexuality that I had never before felt.

Sensuously, like a snake before its entranced prey, she began to dance.

No one dared breathe as the woman silently danced before us. Her hips undulated to the rhythm of some unheard primal music that caressed us with its silence.

Her hands roamed freely over her body as she stroked herself with increasing passion. Her movements flamed a fire within me that seemed to emanate from all of my chakra points at once. But instead of a spiritual fire, this woman was arousing a sexual energy from within us that was as potent and powerful as any astral energies. We were all captivated by her unearthly charms.

The cavern was deathly silent except for the sound of our collective heartbeats. It was as if we had been sealed like insects in amber, forever cut off from the rest of the world.

My Visit To Agharta

In stark contrast to the unearthly silence, the air in the tunnel had become alive with an energy that was almost electrical in nature. I could feel the small hairs on the back of my neck rising in response. At first I thought it was my own inflamed passion for the strange woman before us, but I soon realized that the very atmosphere itself was alive with a raw power that enveloped us all.

So great was our bewitchment that if the gods had decided to strike us dead on the spot, we would have all died in ecstatic joy for having experienced just a glimpse of this enchantress before us.

She stopped moving and slowly brought her arms up, her hands outstretched in an obviously open invitation to join with her, to enjoy the earthly pleasures that she offered so freely, so unselfishly. Her body was a temple, and we were mere mortals, worshipers to her divine body. We were being given a chance to commune with the holy of physical pleasures. To supplicate and be enveloped forever in undescribable ecstasy.

Nothing else mattered to me anymore. My whole purpose in life was to become one with the goddess in front of me. Everything and everyone that ever meant anything to me were forgotten in a blaze of unholy desire.

A GLIMPSE OF HEAVEN AND HELL

Before I could step forward to join the siren before us, our guide, Leo, took a few lurching steps toward the woman. I felt an uncontrollable anger that stabbed and twisted at my heart. Leo was going to take what was rightfully mine. He was going to be the one to adulate at her divine altar, not me. This thought coursed through my blood and filled my brain with fiery anger and hate.

The Master now also moved forwards and I was filled with even more hatred for this man who had been my mentor, my beloved friend for all these years. It was bad enough that the stranger was going to usurp my rightful place with this woman, but now my friend had betrayed me. This was a hurt that struck me to my very core and left me hollow inside and utterly alone.

But Mingyar Dondup was not after the woman, instead he grabbed Leo by his arm and forcibly dragged him back.

My Visit To Agharta

"Come to your senses friend," the Master said, "It's an illusion. She's not real."

"But she wants me," moaned Leo. "She *needs* me. I have to be with her!"

The Master's urgent tone halted my own progress and gave my mind a chance to catch up to the demanding signals of my body. My mind began to clear and I was now aware just how caught up in the moment I had been. I felt that I had been forcibly hypnotized somehow and my mind stripped of all rational thought.

The Master had not released his grip on Leo's arm as he struggled against the Master's grip in an effort to free himself and join his newfound love. However, years of training in the martial arts allowed Mingyar Dondup to hold on to Leo's arm with a firm yet gentle grip. He spoke softly to Leo with soothing words, as a parent might soothingly talk to a small child frightened of the night. Leo soon stopped his protests and began to quietly weep.

"Lobsang," said the Master. "Are you all right? You have to fight it. Don't let it take you. It's a trick."

I didn't answer. My eyes were still riveted to the vision before us. By now she had dropped her arms and regarded us with a blank stare. Her eyes had lost their fire and had become cold and dead, like the glass eyes of an old doll.

Suddenly the air was filled with terrifying shouts and screams in an unknown language. From out of the walls came a group of the most fearsome creatures that I had ever seen before in my life. So loathsome and unbelievable was their appearance that they could have sprung from the worst nightmares of a madman.

They were like the demons from ancient Tibetan legends, but these devils were all too real as they leaped and scuttled about the cavern. The tunnel was now filled with the sickening beasts as they advanced upon us.

Leo had stopped his crying and watched in horror as the monsters filled the cavern.

"It's *them*!" He whispered hoarsely. "They've found us. They know we are here!"

My Visit To Agharta

They came in all shapes and sizes, though all appeared short and stunted due to the twisted shape of their bodies. All were humanoid in structure, but only resembled men in the most perverted of fashions. Their backs were bent and contorted and many carried humps on their shoulders.

Their naked skin was a sickening pale white, like the soft flesh of squirming maggots that swarm the rotting flesh of the dead. Oozing sores and decay covered their skin and it hung in fat folds across their misshapen bodies.

Their faces were the most frightening of all as they revealed their all too human origins. Nevertheless, they were now mutated and degenerate, far removed from their remote human ancestors. Their noses were long and fleshy, almost elephantine in appearance, and their eyes were pig-like and devoid of any trace of humanity. Their contorted mouths were filled with putrid green canine teeth that they obviously used to bite huge chunks out of their victims.

They continued to scream and rage, but instead of attacking us, they fell upon the woman who made no move to protect herself. It was a horrifying sight as the beast-men ripped into her. They ravaged her in unspeakable ways and tore at her flesh with gigantic, yellowed finger nails and decaying teeth.

There was nothing we could do. We were frozen to the spot. Even if we could move, we would have been no match for the evil, blood-crazed creatures. They were totally overwhelming in their numbers and ferocity.

Throughout the ordeal the woman remained strangely silent, even as the creatures ripped her limbs loose and tore at her entrails she uttered not a sound. And just when my fear was at it greatest, when I was certain that my mind was about to shatter and be torn loose forever from its hold on sanity. . .the entire horrifying scene before us vanished.

Save for us, the tunnel was now completely empty. The woman, the creatures, any evidence of their appearance, were now utterly gone. As well, the paralyzing fear and the overwhelming desire had also faded away. The tunnel was silent and peaceful. Only the sounds of our laboured breathing broke the stillness.

"What happened? Where did they go?" I asked, turning to look over my shoulder.

My Visit To Agharta

My Visit To Agharta

"It wasn't real Lobsang," said the Master. "It was an illusion, a vision sent by the hell spawn who have taken and perverted the science and machines of the Old Ones. The creatures you saw were once humans such as us."

Leo sank to his knees and wiped with face with a cloth. He had been the most affected by the vision and his face mirrored the torment in his soul.

"All of my life I had heard the stories," he finally managed to say. "I always thought they were fairy tales told to scare children and hysterical women. I never once thought they could be true. But it is true! The demons really exist and they know we are here."

"Obviously our journey has attracted some unwanted attention," the Master said. "We had better be on our way, just in case our tormenters might want to return and make a physical appearance."

We quickly gathered up our belongings that were dropped during our ordeal and hurried down the tunnel. A thousand questions danced in my head.

"Master," I said. "Surely we must be in the wrong tunnel. How could such a terrible place lead to our beloved Agharta? How could such unholy creatures live so close to the Enlightened Ones and the sacred cities? It doesn't make sense. We must be wrong and this journey is a trick by evil spirits who desire to mislead us."

"It is indeed difficult to imagine why this world would have a need for such loathsome creatures," said the Master. "But they would not be here if they didn't have an important role to play. It is not our place to ask why such things are. We simply have to accept that all is how it should be. But we also have to be diligent in making sure we don't really cross paths with them. It is a fate that I don't particularly relish."

"It has to be the Old Ones' machines," Leo suddenly spoke up. "The ancient machines could do wonderful things like send images across great distances through solid rock. That must be what we saw and felt. We were under the influence of some faraway machine."

"But how could those disgusting animals operate a machine?" I asked.

36

My Visit To Agharta

"The machines must be able to operate on their own, or are so simple that even a child could use them," the Master said. "But as I said before Lobsang, those creatures were once men just as you or I.

"Thousands of years ago they discovered the Old Ones' machines. The machines were still functioning and ready for use. But instead of using these fantastic devices for their original purposes, they used them to control or hurt others. They used the healing rays to inflame their physical pleasures and they abused their bodies and their minds.

"After centuries of continued abuse, the rays slowly changed their genetic structure and they mutated into the hideous beasts we saw today. They have lost most of their intelligence and all of their humanity. They live only for the most disgusting physical pleasures and allow nothing to stand in their way of achieving this."

"Well lets pick up the pace," Leo said. "My village is still quite far away and I want to get us there in one piece."

"No," said the Master. "As much as it distresses me to say, we have another task to deal with first. During our ordeal I received a most disturbing vision. There is an encampment of the beasts nearby and we have to go there."

"That's impossible," Leo countered. "Except for what we just saw, no one has ever seen the beasts around here. They're supposed to live far, far away."

"They are closer than you think," replied the Master. "I suspect that there have been no sightings of the beasts because no one has ever lived to tell of their experience."

I knew that it was pointless to argue with Mingyar Dondup when it came to his visions. He was known all over the land for his abilities and selfless acts. If the Master said that we were needed someplace, then there was no question in my mind on what I had to do.

The Master pointed to a group of boulders against the wall. Moving them aside revealed a small, dark passageway that ran deep into the rock.

My Visit To Agharta

INTO THE DRAGONS LAIR

The secret passage was no more than a fissure through the tunnel wall, barely big enough for one man at a time to enter. The master led the way with Leo watching our backs.

We had walked for no more than ten or fifteen minutes when the fissure opened into a small, dank cavern. The smell was absolutely disgusting. It was all we could do not to bolt and run. The light was dim, consisting of several small fires scattered about on the floor. We could just make out a small enclosure made of rough wood and wire. In this pen I could see the unmoving body of a woman.

"Is that the woman we saw back in the tunnel?" I whispered.

"Shhh," cautioned the Master. "It isn't her. This is a real woman from the surface who needs our help. Look in the back of the cave. There are the beasts that hold her captive."

Straining my eyes against the dim light, I could just barely make out ten or fifteen figures lying up against the cave wall. Even in the dark, I could tell that these were the same types of disgusting creatures that we had seen back in the tunnel. They appeared to be unconscious or asleep.

"Now is the time we must act," said the Master. "They have drugged themselves into a stupor with the rays of a machine. We can get in and out without them knowing we were even here."

With Mingyar Dondup leading the way, we silently entered the cavern and made directly for the enclosure. The women inside was also unconscious and seemed all but lifeless as we pulled down the wires surrounding her. At the same time we kept a watchful eye on the figures on the far side of the cave, ever vigilant to their possible awakening.

With the comatose woman supported between us, we reentered the fissure.

We quickly made it to our starting point in the tunnel and rolled the boulders back into their original place in front of the fissure.

My Visit To Agharta

"We must take her away from this place as quickly as we can," ordered the Master. "The more ground we can put between us and those beasts the safer we will be. The creatures will be slow to awaken from their machine induced state of intoxication so we have time to get away."

"We can take her to my people," Leo said. "She will be safe there."

Using our blankets we made a hammock to carry between us. We placed the still unconscious woman inside and started off down the tunnel.

It was obvious that she had been treated roughly by her captors. She was dirty and covered in scratches and bruises, but I could tell she was no more than 21 or so. What was left of her clothes hung in tatters across her body. I shuddered to think of what unspeakable things had been done during her captivity. I said a silent prayer in her behalf. No doubt my companions were also contemplating the sad figure that was now in our protection.

I have no idea how long we walked. At this point my body and mind were numb from exhaustion and the day's events. If not for my Tibetan training in Yoga and other mystic disciplines, I would have collapsed onto the rock floor many miles back. As it was, I could barely carry my end of the sling that held our unmoving guest. Nevertheless, the journey remained uneventful and the tunnel was as peaceful and quiet as before. This was a welcomed change due to the now fragile condition of our collective psyches.

I would have shouted for joy if I had the strength when Leo finally said that his town was nearby. Instead, I straightened my back and quickened my step, gaining fortitude from the knowledge that at least this part of our trip would soon be at an end.

The tunnel opened into a large cavern and we entered Leo's hometown.

THE GOOD PEOPLE

With the woman in safe hands we were shown to a guest house. Of course when I say "house" a better description would be a yurt, which is a Mongolian structure that is round and portable with a self-supporting frame. These yurts were built from saplings laced together with leather thongs and covered with animal hides. All in all, a very comfortable and welcoming place to stay after days of sleeping on cold, hard rock.

Leo's town consisted of several small groups of yurts clustered in the middle of the cavern. There were probably no more than eighty or ninety people total, most consisting of extended families. These people were essentially nomads who could pick up and move their belongings in short notice.

In the center of the village stood a tall pole carved with figurines. At the apex of this pole was a bright light that illuminated the entire cavern in such a way that I would have sworn the sun was overhead. Somewhere in the past I had heard of such things, old tales of magic crystals that shone with the light of the sun. Considering what I had seen over the last several days, glowing rocks would not seem out of place in this strange land.

After we had settled in, we dined with the rest of the village in a large community hut. We were told by the village matriarch that the woman we had brought in was responding to their herbal treatments and would be able to leave soon.

"When the Good People arrive they will take her with them," the old woman said to us. "She will be given treatments to erase her memories of the caves and of the beast-men. When she is returned to the surface, she will have no memory of where she has been or what has happened to her. It is best that she forget what has happened. No one should carry such memories with them."

"Who are the Good People?" I asked.

"The Good People are those who resisted abusing the Old Ones' machines for their carnal pleasures," Leo answered. "Instead, they are said to be dedicated to doing battle with the beasts and helping those in need. They are the Knights of Agharta who use the machines to help others.

"Like the beasts, I always thought the Good People were fairy tales. Much as the surface world has tales of knights who slew dragons, we have legends of the Knights of Agharta who guard the underworld from destruction and evil. I guess I should have listened more closely to the stories my grandmother used to tell me."

My Visit To Agharta

"The Good People do exist," the Master said. "They have been expecting our arrival and will be here shortly for the woman."

"How do you know this?" Leo asked.

"We have been called to sacred Agharta for more than one reason," Mingyar Dondup said. "Even though my apprentice had no idea of why we were called, it was our responsibility to rescue the woman from the beasts. This act was necessary to cleanse our souls and allow our bodies to accept the different vibrational realm where beloved Agharta exists."

"There is to be a gathering of the enlightened souls from this planet," the Master continued. "Soon will be the time when great changes will take place on Earth. These changes will be the beginning of a great transformation for all of mankind. Much like our rescue of the woman, mankind must learn to let go of its selfish ways and live to help his brothers. We will soon be joined by our brethren from the stars. They have been watching us for a long time, waiting for us to reach the crossroads in our spiritual evolution. When the time is right, we will be invited to join them and see for ourselves the wonders the creator has provided in this universe."

So that was how the Master knew about the woman, I thought to myself. He had been told in advance where we needed to go and what was to be done.

"The Good People will be here when the fire crystal is on its fifth cycle," the Master told the villagers.

"So that's what the light is in the center of town," I said. "What is a fire crystal?"

Leo answered my question: "Fire crystals used to be the power source of the ancient civilisations of Atlantis and Mu. Each crystal contains the energies of a star in their heart and will remain powerful for thousands of years. The ancient crystals were of course much larger and more powerful than ours. It is said that these two great powers used their crystals to wage war and as a consequence destroyed each other at the same time. A few crystal pieces survived the cataclysm, that's how we got ours. We are considered a powerful village because of our fire crystal. There are those who would love to take it away from us and gain our power, but we won't let that happen."

My Visit To Agharta

When our meal was finished we returned to our yurt to rest. There the Master told me about the next leg of our journey.

"When the Good People arrive for the woman, we will go with them as well," he said. "We will be taken to a portal that will allow our physical bodies access to the realm of Agharta. Because of this, we must now fast until we make the transition. I would also suggest you use the remaining time to clear your mind of unpleasant thoughts. In the land of Agharta your thoughts are reality and the untethered mind can be a dangerous thing."

Like its heavenly counterpart, the fire crystal in the center of the village began to slowly grow dimmer to imitate nightfall. Even after centuries of living underground, these people still needed to respond to the ancient dance of the cosmos. Night in the caves with a fire crystal was equivalent to twilight on the surface. It was just dark enough to sleep, yet not so dark that an enemy could sneak up on you when you slept. I did my Yoga exercises and tried to sleep. It would be a restless night.

A HORRIFYING TALE

The next "morning" we were up and ready to go. Both the Master and I were fasting and I could tell that he missed his morning cup of tea just as much, if not more, than I. The entire town had turned out to see us off, and our friend Leo brought with him someone who was also very happy to be there that morning.

"Look who is awake and ready to go," Leo said happily.

To my surprise, Leo had with him the woman who just a few hours ago seemed close to death. Now she was awake and wearing fresh, clean clothes. Her light brown hair was washed and combed, and with the exception of a few light scratches on her face, appeared to be healing quickly.

Smiling broadly, the woman hugged both the Master and myself. "I understand that I also have you two to thank for rescuing me from those monsters," she said.

The Master smiled at the woman and reached out to move a lock of her hair off of her face, much as a doting parent would do with a beloved child.

42

My Visit To Agharta

"That time is past my child," the Master said softly. "It is time for you to begin your journey home and start your life anew."

Over the years I had often seen this soft side of the Master toward others. While many monks and lamas seal themselves away from their fellow man in search of spiritual enlightenment, Mingyar Dondup had always sought out those who needed help, giving freely of himself to those in need. He was often criticized by those who thought he should spend more time at prayer then out helping the sick. But he had once told me that the true path toward enlightenment was more than mastery of the self, It also involved mastery over the ego. The greatest gift that we can give to others is ourselves.

"We will be going with you part of the way my dear," the Master told the woman. "You will be given a chance to rest with the Good People before you are sent home."

A loud roar, like that of a jet, suddenly filled the cavern and the crowd split apart to allow access to the strangest looking vehicle I think I have ever seen. The machine was large and shaped like a cylinder with large openings on all sides. Around each opening was a large rubber cushion that opened down their entire length. The roar came from fans inside each opening. The wind they produced kept the rubber cushions inflated.

Like us, the villagers were in awe of the strange machine in front of them. As Leo had said earlier, the stories of the men-beasts and the Good People were considered folklore and fairy tales, though many of the old people could remember first-hand experiences, the young people laughed it off as tall tales. Everyone wanted to see a legend come to life.

The machine settled down onto the floor of the cavern. From our perspective it resembled somewhat the new hovercraft ferry that operates between Dover and Calais, France. From the side of the craft, a door opened and from within emerged a young man dressed in a white robe who clasped his hands together and bowed to the crowd that had gathered around him.

"I am here to take Master Mingyar Dondup and his group," the man said to the crowd. "Is he here amongst you?"

My Visit To Agharta

We stepped out of the crowd and the Master said: "I am Master Mingyar Dondup. We humbly request a small place on your vessel. We are small in number and would not take up much room or trouble you in any way."

"Welcome Master," the young man greeted. "I would be honored if you and your friends would travel with me. I have far to go and your company would be most welcome."

We shook hands with Leo, thanking him for his help.

"I can't say that it was a fun job," Leo joked, "but it definitely was an adventure, one that I don't think I'd want to repeat again any time soon. Good luck to all of you and may the gods favor you for the rest of your journey."

Along with the woman, we entered the craft and the driver pulled the door shut behind us. The inside of the craft was small compared to overall size. I imagine the fans used to generate the flow of air took up most of the available space. But the inside was warm and the seats comfortable, so we settled back for the next leg of our trip.

"You may call me Toc Hamir," the driver told us. "This vehicle is made specifically to travel the tunnels. That's why it's shaped like a cylinder. The ship floats on cushions of air generated by the fans and we can travel quite fast as long as the tunnels are the right size. For the large tunnels we can only use the bottom fans to float across the floor. But smaller tunnels allow me to use all the fans that surround the ship and increase our speed."

As Toc Hamir busied himself with the controls, the Master handed out chunks of rough bread and cheese given to us by the friendly people of Leo's village. As we ate, our new travelling companion told us how she came to be captured and enslaved by the beast men.

"My name is Alice Runyan and I was born and raised in Austin Texas," she said. "After graduating college I moved to New York City to work for the ******* company. I hadn't been with them for very long when it all happened. I had worked late one night and the building was almost empty. When I got onto the elevator and pushed the lobby button, the elevator instead went all the way down into the basement. I pressed the lobby button again, but the elevator continued to go down past the basement level. When the doors finally opened, I found myself in a large rocky cavern. The elevator refused to work and I was trapped. That's when I saw *them*!"

Alice paused, her eyes glazed over as she remembered the fearful event.

"Go on dear," the Master said kindly. "It will do you good to remember."

Alice bit her lip and shuddered noticeably as she fought back the tears.

It occurred to me as I watched Alice struggle to talk about her ordeal, that she was handling the memory much better than most people would have been able in similar circumstances. I surmised that possibly part of her treatments back in the village consisted of special herbal remedies to help deal with traumatic memories.

Still, Alice managed to continue her recollections.

"The elevator had let me off in a room that looked like it had been blasted out of solid rock," she said. "The only light came from the elevator and it didn't penetrate very far into the darkness. I became aware of a horrible smell, somewhat like garbage and unwashed people. It stank so bad it brought tears to my eyes. There was a whispering sound coming from the darkness in front of me and I backed into the elevator to try and escape. But it didn't do any good. They came right in to me. I couldn't stop them."

"Who came in?" The Master asked her.

"*Them*!" Alice suddenly screamed causing Toc Hamir to turn from his controls and look back at us.

"They were horrible," Alice whispered. "There were three of them. They walked right into the elevator and grabbed me. I couldn't stop them. I had never seen anything like them before in my life. They were short and fat, almost bloated. Their skin was pale white, bristly and covered with dripping sores. But their faces made me want to start screaming and never stop. Their lips hung from their open mouths and they drooled uncontrollably. It looked like their faces were covered with tumors of some kind because they were distorted and twisted in unearthly ways. And although they were almost hidden by the growths, I could see their eyes and they were human eyes."

"I don't really remember too much after that," she said in a voice almost too faint to hear. "I know they stripped me of my clothes and molested me, but everything else is vague. I remember being in a cage, sometimes with other people like me. When the creatures wanted us, they just came and took us and there was nothing we could do. They must have kept me drugged or something because I just didn't care anymore. That's all I remember until you came and rescued me."

"That's fine Alice," the Master said. "It's all over now and you should rest and try to forget."

The Master Mingyar Dondup began to speak to Alice in a quiet, rhythmic voice as he slowly moved his hands above her shoulders and head. I recognized the technique the Master was using to smooth Alice's aura. When we become sick or upset, our astral energy field, or aura, becomes week, ragged and displaced. By using his hands as external energy points, the Master was able to infuse his healing energies into Alice's auric field to hasten her healing and quiet her injured, troubled soul.

Alice soon drifted off to sleep and we moved towards the front of the vessel so we would not disturb her.

"It sounds like she was the victim of the beasts' sex machines," Toc Hamir said to us. "They are able to use the old machines to stimulate the sexual energies of anyone they wish. If you fall victim of the machines rays, all rational thought leaves your mind to be replaced with an animal hunger for sexual pleasure. Many of the beasts live their entire lives under the influence of those machines. They often kidnap people from the surface to become mind controlled sexual victims of their perverted desires."

"What about the other people she said she saw?" I asked.

"They're gone forever," he replied. "I suppose Alice was lucky you came when you did. For you see, the beasts are also cannibals."

My Visit To Agharta

THE GATES OF ETERNITY

We continued swiftly down the tunnels in our incredible machine. Toc Hamir told us that we would be arriving at our destination shortly. However, I still worried about the eventual fate of our new friend Alice.

"Don't worry about her," Toc Hamir said to me. "After I drop you off, I will take her to my people to begin her complete healing. We will use the machines in our possession to heal her tortured body and mind. Then we will remove all memories of the caves and the beast men. She will have no memories of anytime after she got onto that elevator. We will take her back to the surface and secretly leave her at a hospital that works with cases such as hers. She will have some confusion as she tries to deal with her amnesia, but she will recover completely and go on with her life."

Tragic to say, but there are thousands of people who, like Alice, disappear every year seemingly right off the face of the earth. Some do reappear, many suffering from unexplained amnesia. Many, however, are never seen again. Their disappearance remains forever a mystery to those who are left behind. I wonder now how many of these unfortunate souls disappearances were actually unlucky encounters with the underworld beast men.

As I sat and mused over these unpleasant thoughts, our machine slowed noticeably and then came to a complete stop. Our driver politely announced that we had finally arrived at our destination.

By now Alice was awake and thanked us again for our help. As she gave us each a quick hug, she tearfully promised that she would never forget our heroism . This was a promise that we hoped she would not be able to keep.

We stood and bowed in farewell as Toc Hamir restarted the hovercraft and quickly sped away down the tunnel. I said a silent prayer for Alice and hoped the gods would watch and protect her in thc difficult days ahead.

I looked around, suddenly aware of our new environment. The cavern was extremely large, its walls stretched upwards to finally disappear into the darkness with no ceiling in sight. In front of us was a brightly glowing vertical whirlpool of

My Visit To Agharta

light and mist, large enough to drive a tram through. Around it were a number of people who were following a golden path on the floor of the cavern. This path led straight into the heart of the whirlpool.

"This is the etherial entrance to sacred Agharta, Lobsang," the Master said to me. "This is the passageway through time and space that connects the inner world with ours. The center of our planet is more than a hollow space within a sphere. This space actually transcends physical reality and exists simultaneously in a number of different dimensions and realities. Once we enter the dimensional vortex our vibrational field will be increased to match the higher level of Agharta. Only through this method are physical beings such as ourselves able to enter Agharta."

"Why are these other people here Master?" I asked.

"They are all here like us Lobsang," the Master replied. "We have all been called to Agharta for an important task. It is an important time for us all as such gatherings of the great minds of the universe is a rare occasion indeed."

We stepped onto the path which gleamed with the elegance of pure, regal gold. All around us were thousands, probably millions of beings of every shape and size. Some were human and others obviously were not. It appeared that there were representatives from every intelligent species in the universe in this cavern making their way towards the vortex.

"These are the enlightened souls of this universe Lobsang," said the Master. "Like ourselves, all have been chosen and touched by the divine light that is the Creator of all that is. We are the representatives of the ultimate consciousness in which all life emanates. It is through us that others will learn of their true selves and purpose."

All around us was the contingent of human enlightened souls, all arriving at the same time to make their way toward the light. I could see with us many of the greatest minds that had ever walked on the earth. Others I didn't recognize but I knew intuitively that they would live and teach in future times. But time had no meaning in this place as all eras are brought together as one.

"We are now walking on the path of life," the Master said referring to the golden lane under our feet. "It is this path that all who live in the physical world will someday have to walk when they leave their corporeal bodies."

I was in awe of all the great people who were now walking with me. I recognized Siddhartha Gotama, known as the Buddha, and the prophet Zarathushtra who founded Zoroastrianism. Lalleshwari, or Lall of India who under the tutelage of Shrii Siddhanath, attained God-realization, and became one of the most celebrated of spiritual poets. There was Emanuel Swedenborg, the noted Swedish scientist, philosopher and theologian, and Madame H. P. Blavatsky, founder of the Theosophical Movement.

Still the great souls of planet Earth continued to walk before me. There was Sabbatai Zevi, the Jewish mystic and founder of the Sabbatean sect. Jeanne D'Arc, known as Joan of Arc, French saint and national heroine. Comte de Saint-Germain, who Voltaire said was "a man who knows everything and who never dies." There was also the French astrologer Michel de Nostradame and Éliphas Lévi, a leader of the occult revival in the 1800's.

These enlightened souls and countless other spiritual teachers from throughout the past, present and future were all here representing the best from planet Earth. I was humbled to be included with this congregate.

The portal was now before us. Its spiritual energies separated our world from that of Agharta as its swirling vortex drew us in collectively.

We travelled beyond time and space aware of not only ourselves, but of the billions of souls that journeyed along side us. We were one.

SACRED AGHARTA

In less time than it took to form a single thought, we reemerged from the other side of the vortex. We were no longer in the cavern and the tableau in front of me was so incredible it was almost more than my mind could bear.

We had emerged on the side of a great mountain. From this peak there flowed a great river of enlightened beings who now glowed with the divine light of creation that permeated this sacred land. At the base of the mountain was a vast plain already filled with billions of travelers such as ourselves and more continued to stream down the mountain to join their brethren.

From our perspective it appeared as if we were standing in the middle of a great bowl of fantastic size. Instead of a horizon, the land curved upwards and away from us in all directions to finally become lost in the turquoise blue sky above. In the center of the sky there hung a sun of magnificent beauty. Somewhat smaller and dimmer than the sun of our solar system, but still casting a splendid soft, golden brightness that illuminated the entire landscape with its holy luminance.

The land was rich in beauty and life. In an almost tropical environment, flowers of all types grew in profusion throughout. Their perfume wafted on the breeze bringing an almost childlike delight to my sense of smell as I remembered sweet days of youth. Streams of crystal clear water flowed and bubbled through the forests and grasslands. The air was alive with the sounds of birds and insects whose songs rose and fell with the universal rhythm of all life. In the distance I could see great and beautiful cities with buildings that seemed to defy the law of gravity. The structures, which gave the appearance of being made from beautiful clear crystal and gemstones, glowed with the incredibly radiant light of cosmic grandeur.

Until he spoke up, I had almost forgotten the Master who stood beside me equally in awe of the sight before us.

"Behold," he said magnificently. "Sacred Agharta."

Many believe that Agharta is a city in the center of the Earth. However, Agharta is actually the name of the entire land and not one single city. Here resides Earths cosmic power. All powers of matter, energy and time-space dimensions achieved by living creatures, originate from this cosmic source. In this land live a number of races with disparate cultures and traditions. They live in a much more evolved and advanced dimension compared with human life on the surface, in perfect symbiosis with the planet and its living reality.

Other races other than those from Earth also occupy the interdimensional land of Agartha. Here there are large colonies of extraterrestrial peoples originating from many diverse places in our universe. These groups also interrelate at different dimensional levels.

My Visit To Agharta

My Visit To Agharta

The capital of Agharta is the etheric city of Shamballa. This city is the highest expression of this internal civilisation and vibrates at astral frequencies. There, the creative idea and the astral program for the Earths evolution are conceived and instituted. In Shamballa dwell extraordinary beings who vibrate at the highest frequencies of the universe. They are free beings, owners of life. They build destiny. They live together in large clans, guided by the Elders. The eldest clan is the keeper of the Word. The elder of this clan is the Directing Mind of all life inside and outside the planet.

They exist on higher frequencies, totally free of the temporal system. Going through time planes, they are subjected to their effects only so long as they are immersed in them. But their entity remains unchanged in its immortal nature. They are the Alpha and Omega of all life in the universe.

They wear rich, light clothing of encompassed beauty and art, laced with gold and multicolored arabesques. They are taller than the average human with strong and extremely vital features that could be likened to those of the Polynesian people.

Unfortunately, we were not pure enough to visit Shamballa. Even though we were able to transcend our surface world vibrational state and enter Agharta, we were still far removed from those pure souls who dwelt in Shamballa. But our reason for being here was not for sightseeing. We had another purpose, a purpose that was soon to be revealed to all.

We joined the multitude of enlightened beings who had collected on the great plain at the foot of the dimensional doorway. Above us in the sky soared great spherical vessels that dipped and dodged in the breeze like the kites of Lhasa.

"Look in the sky," the Master pointed out. "Those are soul crafts made up of pure thought and capable of travelling anywhere in this universe."

The air was vibrant with excitement as the sound of billions of voices drifted over the landscape. All who were here knew that this was a momentous occasion in the history of the present universe and felt honored and humble to be a part of it.

"Incredible, there are so many," I said out loud. "The world can scarcely hold us all."

My Visit To Agharta

The Master laughed a rich, deep laugh of utter joy and delight, something that I had never heard him do in all the years that I knew him on the surface world.

"Look around us Lobsang," the Master said as he spread out his arms. "Beings from all worlds and all times have come together at this one point in infinite time and space. It is a miracle that I had scarcely dreamt possible, yet here we all are. But you shouldn't worry about Agharta overflowing with enlightened beings, because this place sits in the center of both the material and astral planes of existence. Not only is it located in the center of our planet, it is also located in the centers of millions of other planets. Agharta is in the heart of all conscious beings throughout the universe."

A MESSAGE FOR ALL MANKIND

Suddenly, the air around us sparkled and shimmered as a great presence moved through the multidimensional reality that was Agharta. All voices in the land were suddenly silent and every head looked upward toward the great sun that shone over the world. It was as if all of creation was silent and waiting for what would come next.

As we watched, the sun started to rapidly spin in the heavens, at the same time throwing off great streamers of brilliant colour. To me the sun looked like a great pearl in the sky, spinning on its own axis with multicoloured rays of light shooting off it in all directions.

The entire world was bathed in an iridescent light of sublime beauty that sent a collective feeling of peace and love through all who were there. No one dared move for fear of missing even a moment of this spectacular event.

And then, just when it seemed the sun could spin no faster, it abruptly broke free from its place in the heavens and appeared to fall straight for us. Many upon seeing such a phenomenon would have fled in terror. However, the air was filled with such peace and joy, that it was impossible for fear to gain a foothold. Instead, we were awestruck at the magnitude of the entire event.

The rapidly spinning sun fell closer toward us. Its rainbow beauty seemed to fill the entire sky with its grandeur as it swooped low over the landscape. But then

53

when it seemed as if it would crush the entire world, it stopped and began to slowly back away until it was back in its original position in the center of the sky. However, it continued to spin in place, casting a wondrous golden light on all that surrounded it.

This light was the purest essence of peace and love, and with it came a consciousness that filled my entire being with its glory. As it did, I became aware of the thoughts and feelings of everyone that had been called to Agharta at this moment. We were all connected by the love and hope that was this consciousness, and I intuitively knew that this was the Ultimate Consciousness that was beyond the multiverse. This was the Creator of all.

Tears of joy sprang from my eyes and ran freely down my cheeks as its glorious voice rang out and addressed all who were in its presence. It spoke to us collectively and individually at the same time. We were many, from different times and worlds, yet the Creator acknowledged us all.

"It fills my being with happiness that you could be here with me today Lobsang," the voice said to me. "This happiness fills all who are part of my creation with the transcendent love that is my creative force."

I looked over at the Master. From the ecstatic look on his face he was obviously hearing the same thing that I was hearing, a collective message, yet personalized for his ears only.

"Lobsang," the voice continued. "You are an essential part of the message that must be taken back for all of mankind to hear. There are other representatives from different times on Earth who are also responsible for delivering my message to their own time. Each message is important for each world and time. Yet all contain the same underlying truth that is necessary for all to hear and know.

"Know that the planet Earth is far older then your science dare imagine. Your planet is one of the chosen worlds that has survived the birth and death of numerous universes. These chosen planets are the ultimate sanctuaries of evolved life and consciousness. These shining beings carry with them the knowledge of past universes in order to continue my creation. Your universe is just one of an infinite number of universes in the cosmic foam of my foundation. Each universe is born from the nothingness that is my being. It is consciousness that compels each universe to evolve living things that become points of light in the fabric of time and space. These nodes of consciousness are the perfect expression of my creation.

"Each universe has a time to be born, to live, to die and to be reborn again. Just as all life is born, lives, dies and is reborn again. Each universe expands from its point of inception bringing with it the cosmic energy that drives the engine of creation. When a universe can expand no further, it doesn't collapse back onto itself, instead the wall of tension in space and time that separates each universe from each other snaps like a rubber band. This burst in time and space creates a singularity from which a new universe is born from the nothingness that is the foundation of creation.

"The ultimate beings of thought and light, in order to transfer knowledge from one universe to another, have taken numerous worlds under their care, and with astral energies that exist both in the multiverse and in the planes of existence beyond, have enabled these worlds to survive the death of thousands of past universes and they will endure the passing of many more. Your home, the planet Earth is one of the chosen planets. It has seen the birth and death of many universes. It is precious to my creation.

"Your species is one of many that have arisen from the womb of mother Earth. Humans have evolved according to my divine plan. Just as you are born an infant and grow into adulthood, so is it with all forms of life and diversity of the species. They start from the simplest expressions of life and grow to become more developed and complex to receive intelligence to compliment their consciousness.

"Humans have evolved and achieved intelligence and understanding of free will. You are a part of the material world and a part of the spirit world. Not all intelligent species develop their spiritual aspect. Some never grasp the astral worlds that exist beyond the multiverse. Because of this they are constantly reborn into the physical until their species develops their spiritual and astral sides. This is where your people are needed T. Lobsang Rampa.

"The human race was born on Earth, one of my blessed planets. It is the destiny of your species to spiritually evolve to become Beings of Light. As with other Beings of Light, you will guide other species throughout this universe, and other universes, to also evolve spiritually. As your people through history have looked upon these guides as angels, so will others look upon your race. It is a momentous task that I have given your people. But I would not have done so if the human race was not capable.

"However, as a species, the human race is still in its infancy. You are reaching a critical time in your development where you can either fulfill your destiny, or die and become reabsorbed into the cosmic dust of my creation. The choice is up to you. You are capable of knowing the universal love and forgiveness that is my law. Yet you are also adept of such hate and destruction that it is imperative that you learn to grow beyond these petty emotions and take your place as honored members of the universal community.

"This I will tell you of the upcoming days of your people. Many live in fear now of the potential nuclear destruction that certain countries threaten each other with. However, the countries that now make up the Soviet Union will soon abandon their oppressive and spiritually sterile ways. Many countries that have suffered under this iron hand will find themselves free for the first time in many years. But this freedom comes with a price. Because of the abrupt way that the Soviet Union will collapse, many countries who were dependent on economic support will be forced to fend for themselves. This will cause great suffering with the innocents who are far removed from world politics.

"I will say to you Lobsang that despite the changes in the upcoming years, your beloved Tibet will continue to be subjugated by China. As the years pass China will be less interested in ruling Tibet with an iron fist and instead will allow the people more determination of their own fate. However, Tibet will not be free from Chinese rule in your lifetime.

"Because of planet wide political changes, the world will breathe a little easier from the fear of atomic death from the skies. But a new enemy of truth and enlightenment will emerge in the days just before and after the new millennium. This enemy will arise as religious fundamentalism and extremism.

"Numerous people who feel oppressed by the world situation will turn to religion in search of answers. However, there are men and woman who crave power and material wealth who will exploit these people and pervert their spiritual quest with dogmas of hate and destruction. The religions of the cross and the crescent moon will be the birthing fields of these new enemies of mankind. These wretched souls will be sent out to do evil, convinced that they are fulfilling God's will.

"Many good men and women will fall under the spell of this type of religious abomination. They will interpret their holy books to fit their twisted ideals. They will suffer from the sin of pride as they declare only themselves fit to live in the Creator's world. They will oppress the weak and those who are different, robbing them of their freedom and even their lives. They will demand governments based on only their religious beliefs, using fear and death to enforce their will. And again, perverting the name of the Creator to justify their evil.

"Multiple governments will fall and be replaced by theocracies. These Church-States will declare themselves exclusively beloved by the Creator as they pass laws to permanently rid themselves of those they deem undesirable. A new genocidal madness will sweep the planet as my beloved innocents are killed by these evil forces. Those whose religious beliefs differ will be killed. Those who disagree politically will be killed. Women, who are equal in my eyes, will be forced to be subservient to men. Those whose sexual natures are considered different or abnormal will be murdered.

"Mankind will suffer great indignities from those who say they are doing God's will, when instead, these people actually worship at the altar of material desires such as power, greed, hatred and perversity. They create false idols of weapons saying it is their right to protect themselves, when in reality they thirst for the blood of their fellow humans. They wrap themselves in cloaks of nationalism and religion, declaring how great and beautiful they are. But in truth, they are but insects who corrupt the true way of universal love and truth for their own selfish needs.

"The Earth will also experience a resurgence of contacts with creatures not of your world. Those races who are the Watchers over mankind work in secret to help guide you onto the correct path of evolution. But others will appear who come from other worlds both in time, space and interdimensionally.

"These beings are intelligent creatures who have failed to discover their spiritual side. They live only for the material universe and know not of the astral planes. They are attracted to humans like moths to a flame. They sense your divine nature and seek to understand and exploit it for their benefit. They will come and take you in your sleep caring not of the emotional and physical scars they leave behind.

"These beings will remain unknown to you as they hide from all sight. The creatures that fly the crafts and do the actual contacts are nothing more than biological constructions of these otherworldly races. These constructions are living creatures born of science whose sole purpose is to travel to other worlds and follow the orders of their masters.

"The mystery of what is now called 'UFOs' will never be solved because of the secretive nature of the beings who are drawn to Earth. Nevertheless, it is the destiny of humans to continue their relationship with these otherworldly entities. It is species such as these that will depend on spiritually evolved humans to awaken the slumbering spirit within them. Mankind will be the Watchers over these races who may currently be superior intellectually over humans, but are inferior spiritually."

"It is your duty Lobsang to take this message to the people of your time. However, you must wait until the designated time to release my words. Only at the right time will mankind be open to hear these words. It will take many years of human time for mankind to heed my message and grow as the spiritual beings they are. If you as a species can prosper through the rough days ahead, your future will be wondrous, not only for you, but also for the thousands of species throughout time and space that humans as Beings of Light will guide to their spiritual evolution. Your people and the other enlightened beings who are here will help create new universes. The choice is up to you."

FAREWELL TO AGHARTA

With those final words, the golden light that surrounded us withdrew and the creative conscious force moved back through the threshold that separated this world from the ultimate reality. The sun, with one final burst of glorious holy light, ceased its spinning and returned to normal.

A collective sigh rose up over the land as a billion souls marveled in the miracle that had just transpired. The voice had spoken to all at the same time, delivering a message that had personal meaning for each as well as a call to duty for all. We

My Visit To Agharta

were to be Beings of Light, those who watch and give guidance to races who are ready to evolve spiritually. I thought about the beings we called angels in our holy writings and wondered what ancient race they may have originated from.

The Master Mingyar Dondup clasped my shoulder, his face beaming with a new fire that burned within his soul. I suspected that my own face was equally radiant. Throughout the land everyone was turning and greeting his neighbor in solidarity. The love and understanding that now filled us was the ultimate connective force of creation. I now understood the simple message that we were expected to take with us and spread throughout the universe.

It may sound simplistic, but the answer to all questions is love. This is the true creative force in the multiverse and the worlds beyond. As the Rev. Emmanual Swedenborg so eloquently put it, "All people who live good lives, no matter what their religion, will have a place in heaven."

I looked out over the vast and mysterious land of Agharta, at the billions of beings from throughout time and space and wondered about their own worlds and the missions they would carry out. Would we ever know their experiences?

"We will someday Lobsang," the Master said, obviously reading my mind.

"The time will come when we will all be together again," said the Master. "We will have much to do with not only this universe, but the many that will come afterwards. It is a wondrous challenge that has been issued to mankind. I know in my heart that we will rise to the occasion and join our fellow enlightened beings in the cosmic dance of eternity."

The sky was now filled with a great multitude of soul crafts that seemingly appeared from out of nowhere. Their shining beauty reflected the light that now blazed from the great mass of beings whose souls glowed with the inner fire of the Creator.

"It is now time for us to leave Lobsang," the Master said sadly.

My heart ached at the thought of leaving this wonderful land. But I knew in my heart that I had to carry forth the message that had been conveyed to us all. It was

60

My Visit To Agharta

our responsibility now, all of us, conscious beings from different worlds in time and space with a simple message of love, forgiveness and the recognition and discovery of our true divine nature. We had an important message to deliver and it was imperative that we set off straight away to administer it.

The soul crafts were now landing to pick up the newly chosen emissaries of the Creator's message. We would all be taken back to our own worlds and times by these magnificent vehicles of pure thought and energy.

It was an awesome sight to see the sky filled with these magnificent vehicles as they received their charges and disappeared high into the heavens. A great feeling of overwhelming peace and honor swelled up into my being as I considered the majesty of what was being played out before me.

Now a great shining craft appeared before us and hovered inches above the ground. It was our turn to leave. I shook hands with the others from Earth who had stood with us. Like us, these great souls would return to their own time to spread the message as it would fit their era.

We entered the vehicle and it immediately took to the air to join the thousands of other soul craft that filled the sky like milkweed seeds on a summer breeze. High into the air we shot, free of the bounds of gravity. At this altitude I could see even clearer the shape of Agharta as a great bowl. This was of course an illusion as we were in the hollowed out center of the Earth. But not just Earth – Agharta's reality stretched beyond our planet and into a multitude of other planets whose hollow exteriors also contained Agharta.

We shot past the great sun and drew closer to the opposite side of the hollow globe. Our craft travelled rapidly over mountains, forests, rivers and seas. Other soul craft flew along side us in the clear atmosphere. We were like children at play with a wonderful new toy. Our mutual joy complimented the light energy that made up the character of our vehicles.

In the distance there appeared a great city. As we rapidly approached I could see great crystal structures stretching high into the air. Their amazingly delicate appearance would have been appropriate for any children's fairy tale or the dreams of the romantic. The entire city shone with a rainbow light that glowed from deep

My Visit To Agharta

within. Huge searchlights of various colours stabbed into the air, looking like fantastic pillars of incredible stone that outshone even the eternal light of the great interior sun.

I had heard about this wondrous city before. A city of crystal towers, pyramids and rainbow lights. This was the Rainbow City, the ancient center of culture whose libraries contain the vast knowledge of millions of different worlds and times.

Our soul craft slowed and came to a stop on the outskirts of the city. The Master turned to me and gently grasped my hands.

"This is where we must part ways Lobsang," he said. "My destiny takes me on a different path than yours. I am to remain here in the Rainbow City to study with the great Masters of Agharta."

"But Master," I said. "We have seen and heard so much. Clearly I can't carry this all back alone. Who will be there to help me but you?"

The Master smiled at me. We had been friends for so long that he already knew my questions before they were even spoken.

"You will not be alone my dear friend," he said kindly. "You will never be alone. We will see each other again soon. This I can promise to you. For your journeys are not yet over. There will be other times when we will be together to explore the mysteries of our universe. There is much that we must do and see. But that is for another time and another place. Now we must go our separate ways and do what we have been asked to do."

He gave my hands one last loving squeeze and he departed the craft. Outside the vehicle, The Master Mingyar Dondup stood on a silver road that entered into the Rainbow City. From the city I could see a procession heading our way to greet their new arrival.

As the soul craft slowly floated up, the Master clasped his hands together and bowed a final farewell to me. I was saddened by his departure, but I was also excited for him and the wonderful adventures that awaited him in the days ahead. I looked forward to hearing of his tales someday when we would be together again.

My Visit To Agharta

The soul craft soared upward once again and sacred Agharta blurred away into nothingness. The deep, clear blue sky was replaced by velvet blackness sprinkled with diamond stars that filled the heavens above Earth. I was floating high above the planet, clear of its atmosphere and free of its gravity. It was the perfect place to sit for awhile and contemplate not only the events over the last few days, but also the events that awaited me in future days.

I thought about the days just past, the people we had met, the beauties and ugliness we had seen. So much had happened in such a short time that it would take weeks for my mind to process it all.

I wondered about Alice Runyan and the days of reconditioning that lay ahead of her. I made a mental note to try to somehow keep abreast of her progress after she was returned to the surface.

I considered the beasts who had kidnaped Alice, and simply for their twisted pleasures, tortured thousands of others throughout the planet. Humans' were truly oddities in this universe. We were capable of so much love and beauty. Yet, as the men-beasts of the caverns showed, we were also capable of much evil and ugliness.

Try as I could, it was almost impossible for me to imagine that we could ever become the angelic Beings of Light that the creative force said was his desired goal. This is a future full of hope and promise that contrasts sharply with those who feel that mankind is doomed to eventual extinction. Few can imagine that they have a spark of the divine within their souls – a spark that under the right conditions, can be fanned into the flame of ultimate creation.

It is our responsibility to ensure that mankind lives up to its true potential. For not only is our survival dependant on this, but the survival of millions of others who live throughout the multiverse is also dependant on our development. For mankind, evolved into Beings of Light, will guide others out of the primeval ooze and into the wonders of our universe that is the birthright of all.

But that time was still ahead – I had the soul craft at my disposal for a little while still. And as the Earth rushed away and the cosmos opened to me, I enjoyed the freedom and bliss of eternity for a while longer. The stars would one day be our home, but for now I would be content just to visit.

My Visit To Agharta

My Visit To Agharta

THE LONG LOST BOOKS OF RAMPA
Section Two
As it Was

In *AS IT WAS*, Rampa writes about transmigration and his own experience in transmigrating into the body of an Englishman who wanted to commit suicide. Rampa also talks about cats, the lives they lived in ancient days and their spiritual connection with Humans

I remember one elderly monk, or I should say lama, who was giving us a lecture, and then he got on to the subject of transmigration.

"In the days of long ago," he said, "in fact long before recorded history began, giants walked upon the Earth. They were the Gardeners of the Earth, those who came here to supervise the development of life on this planet, because we are not the first round of existence here, you know, but like gardeners clearing a plot of land – all life had been removed and then we, the human race, had been left here to make our own way, to make our own development." He stopped and looked around to see if his pupils were at all interested in the subject, which he was propounding. To his gratified astonishment he found that people were indeed deeply interested in his remarks.

"The Race of Giants," he went on, "were not very suitable for life on Earth, and so by magical means the Race of Giants shrank until they were the same size as humans, thus they were able to mingle with humans without being recognized as the Gardeners. But it was often necessary for a different senior Gardener to come and carry out special tasks, it took too long to have a boy born to a woman and then wait out the years of his babyhood and childhood and teenage. So the science of the Gardeners of the Earth had a different system; they grew certain bodies and made sure that those bodies would be compatible with the spirit who would later inhabit them."

A boy sitting in the front suddenly spoke up: "How could a spirit inhabit another person?" The lama teacher smiled upon him and said, "I was just about to tell

65

you. But the Gardeners of the Earth permitted certain men and women to mate so that a child was born to each, and the growth of that child would be most carefully supervised throughout, perhaps, the first fifteen or twenty or thirty years of life.

"Then there would come a time when a highly placed Gardener would need to come to Earth within a matter of days or even hours, so helpers would place the trained body into a trance. Helpers in the astral world would come to the living body, together with the entity who wanted to go to Earth, with their special knowledge they could detach the Silver Cord and connect in its place the Silver Cord of the entity who was the Gardener of the Earth coming to the Earth. The host would then become the vehicle of the Gardener of the Earth, and the astral body of the host would go away to the astral world just as he would do in the case of a person who had died.

"This is called transmigration, the migration of one entity into the body of another. The body taken over is known as the host, and it has been known throughout history, it was practiced extensively in Egypt and it gave rise to what is known as embalming because in those days in Egypt there were quite a number of bodies kept in a state of suspended animation, they were living but unmoving, they were ready for occupancy by higher entities just as we keep ponies waiting for a monk or lama to mount the animal and ride off somewhere."

"Oh my!" exclaimed one boy, "I expect friends of the host were mightily surprised when the body awakened and the one they had thought of as their friend in the past was possessed of all knowledge. My! I wouldn't like to be a host, it must be a terrible feeling to have someone else take over one's body."

The teacher laughed and said, "It would certainly be a unique experience. People still do it. Bodies are still prepared, specially raised so that if the need arises a different entity can take over a fresh body – if it becomes necessary for the good of the world as a whole."

For days after the boys had discussed it, and in the way of boys, some of them pretended that they were going to be taking over bodies. But to me, thinking back on that dread prediction, it was no joke, it wasn't amusing to me, it was an ordeal to even think about it. It was a continual shock to my system, so great a shock that at times I thought I would go insane.

My Visit To Agharta

CATS - AND THEIR ANCESTORS IN THE PAST

One tutor in particular was intrigued by my love of cats, and the cats' obvious love for me. The tutor knew full well that cats and I conversed telepathically. One day after school hours he was in a very good mood indeed, and he saw me lying on the ground with four or five of our temple cats sitting on me.

He laughed at the sight and bade me accompany him to his room, which I did with some apprehension because in those days a summons to a lama's quarters usually meant a reprimand for something done or not done, or extra tasks to be accomplished. So I followed him at a respectful distance, and once in his rooms he told me to sit down while he talked to me about cats.

"Cats," he said, "are now small creatures, and they cannot speak in the human tongue but only by telepathy. Many, many years ago, before this particular Round of Existence, cats populated the Earth. They were bigger, they were almost as big as our ponies, they talked to each other, they could do things with their forepaws, which then they called hands. They engaged in horticulture and they were largely vegetarian cats.

"They lived among the trees and their houses were in the great trees. Some of the trees were very different from those we now know upon the Earth, some of them, in fact, had great hollows in them like caves, and in those hollows, or caves, the cats made their homes. They were warm, they were protected by the living entity of the tree, and altogether they were a very congenial community. But one cannot have perfection with any species because unless there is some competition, unless there is some dissatisfaction to spur one on, then the creature having such euphoria degenerates."

He smiled at the cats who had followed me and who were now sitting around me, and then he went on, "Such happened to our brothers and sisters cat. They were too happy, too contented, they had nothing to spur their ambition, nothing to drive them on to greater heights. They had no thought except that they were happy. They were like those poor people we saw recently who were bereft of sanity, they were content just to lie beneath the trees and let the affairs of the day take care of themselves. They were static, and so being static they were a failure. As such the Gardeners of the Earth rooted them out as though they were weeds and the earth was allowed to lie fallow for a time. And in the course of time the Earth had reached such a stage of ripeness that again it could be restocked with a different type of entity.

But the cats – well, their fault had been that they had done nothing, neither good nor bad. And so they were sent down again as small creatures like those we see here, they were sent to learn a lesson, they were sent with the inner knowledge that they had once, a very long, long time ago, had been the dominant species on Earth, so they were reserved, very careful to whom they gave their friendship. So to have cats as your friends is a very good thing and something to be cherished.

"They were sent to do a task, the task of watching humans and reporting the progress or the failures of humans so that when the next Round came, much information would have been provided by cats. Cats can go anywhere, they can see anything, they can hear anything, and, not being able to tell a lie, they would record everything precisely as it occurred."

I know that I was quite frightened for the time being! I wondered what the cats were reporting about me. But then one old tom, a champion of many a fight, gave a "Rrrr" and jumped on my shoulders and butted his head against mine, so I knew everything was all right and they would not report me too badly.

TRANSMIGRATION INTO THE BODY OF AN ENGLISHMAN

After a difficult life full of adventure and hardships, my physical body was exhausted and sick. I had travelled to New York city in the United States in an attempt to find proper medical attention. I knew that I was not long for this physical life – but I was determined to live as long as I possibly could in order to complete my mission on Earth.

During my exhaustion, while the physical body was repairing itself, I made an astral journey and saw my beloved Guide and friend, the Lama Mingyar Dondup. He said to me, "Your sufferings have truly been great, too great Lobsang. Your sufferings have been the sour fruit of man's inhumanity to Man, but your body is getting worn out and soon you will have to undergo the ceremony of transmigration."

In the astral world I sat and my companion sat with me. I was told more.

My Visit To Agharta

"Your present body is in a state of collapse, the life of that body will not continue much longer. We feared that such conditions would prevail in the wild Western world that you would be impaired, and so we have been looking about for a body which you could take over and which in time – would reproduce all your own features.

"We have determined that there is such a person. His body is on a very low harmonic of your own, otherwise, of course, a change could not take place. The bodies must be compatible, and this person has a body, which is compatible. We have approached him in the astral, because we saw that he contemplated suicide. It is a young Englishman who is very dissatisfied with life, he is not at all happy, and for some time he has been trying to decide on the most painless method of what he calls 'self-destruction.' He is perfectly willing to leave his body and journey here to the astral world provided he doesn't lose by it!

"We persuaded him a little time ago to change his name to that which you are now using, so there are a few more things to be settled and then you will have to change bodies."

By now my health was deteriorating very rapidly, and there were serious fears that I would not live long enough to undergo the ceremony of transmigration. I was finally told one day that I should journey into the astral and meet the astral body of the man whose physical vehicle I was going to take over.

For the present I rested, and mused upon the problems of transmigration. This person's body was not of much use to me because it was HIS body and had a lot of vibrations incompatible with my own. In time, I was told, the body would conform exactly to my own body when at that same age, and if Westerners find this a difficult matter to believe or understand, let me put it like this. The Western world knows about electro-plating, and the Western world also knows about electro-typing. In the latter system an article can be immersed in a certain fluid and a special "connector" is applied opposite the article, and when current is turned on at the correct rate and amperage, an exact duplicate of the original item is built up. This is known as electro-typing.

Again, it is possible to do electro-plating. One can plate in a variety of metals; nickel, chromium, rhodium, copper, silver, gold, platinum, etcetera. One merely has to know how to do it. But the current flows from one pole to another through a liquid, and the molecules of one pole are transferred to the other pole. It is a simple enough system, but this is not a treatise on electro-plating. Transmigration and the replacing molecule by molecule of the "fabric" of the host, by that of the new occupant is very real, it has been done time after time by those who know how.

Fortunately those who know how have always been people of reliable character, otherwise it would be a terrible thing indeed if one did just take over another person's body and do harm. I felt rather smug, foolishly so perhaps, when I thought that – well, I am going to do good, I don't want to take over anyone else's silly body, all I want is peace. But it seemed there was to be no peace in my life.

In passing, and as one who has studied all religions, I must point out that Adepts did it for life after life. The Dalai Lama himself had done so, and the body of Jesus was taken over, and it had been common knowledge even in the Christian belief until it was banned because it made people too complacent.

That night I once again left my body to travel to the astral planes. I realized that I was being called from a great distance and my astral self answered this call where I found myself in beautiful surroundings. In the trees birds sang, birds of a type which I had not seen on Earth for these were glorious creatures indeed, birds of many different colours, birds of many different plumage.

I walked on among the trees, and then I came to an open space which was indeed a garden, a garden of brilliant flowers, none of a type that could be recognized by me. The flowers seemed to nod toward me as if in greeting. In the distance I could see people wandering about as if they were luxuriating in this glorious garden. Every so often a person would bend and sniff a flower. At times others would reach up skywards, and a bird would come and land on his outstretched hand. There was no fear here, only peace and contentment.

I walked on a while, and then before me I saw what seemed to be an immense temple. It had a cupola of shining gold and the walls which supported it were of a light fawn colour. Other buildings stretched away from it, each in a pastel shade, all in harmony, but at the entrance to the temple, a group of people were waiting. Some of them wore the robes of Tibet, and another – I could not understand what he was wearing for the moment, it looked as if he was wearing black or something very

My Visit To Agharta

dark. And then I saw as we approached, that it was a man of the Western world attired in a Western raincoat.

At my approach the lamas turned and spread their hands in our direction, spread their hands in welcome. I saw that one of them was my Guide and friend, the Lama Mingyar Dondup, so I knew that all would be well for this man was good and good only. Another figure I saw was even more eminent when upon the earthy plane, but now he was just one of the welcoming "committee" awaiting us.

Our happy greetings were soon exchanged, and then as one we moved into the body of the great temple, traversing the central hall and moving further into that building. We entered a small room the existence of which was not easy to discern, it appeared as if the walls slid away and, admitting us to its presence, closed solidly behind us.

My Guide, obviously the spokesman, turned to me and said, "My brother, there is the young man whose body you are going to inhabit." I turned and faced the young man aghast. Certainly there was no resemblance at all between us, he was much smaller than I, and the only resemblance between us was that he was bald the same as I! My Guide laughed at me and shook an admonitory finger at my nose: "Now, now, Lobsang," he laughed, "not so quick with your decisions. All this has been planned, first I am going to show you some pictures from the Akashic Record." And this he did.

Upon completing our viewing of the Record he said, addressing the young man, "Now young man, I think it is time that you told us something about yourself, for if one is to take over your body then it certainly is time for the one taking over to know that with which he is faced."

The young man, so addressed, looked very truculent indeed and replied in sullen tones, "Well, no, I have nothing to say about my past, it has always been held against me. Whatever I do say about my past it will only be used to pull me down."

My Guide looked sadly at him and said, "Young man, we here have vast experience of these things and we do not judge a man by what his parentage is alleged to be, but what that man is himself."

My Visit To Agharta

My Guide sighed and then said, "You were going to commit the mortal sin of suicide, a sin indeed, a sin which could have cost you dear in many lives of hardship to atone. We offer you peace, peace in the astral, so that you may gain understanding of some of those things, which have troubled you throughout your life. The more you cooperate, the more easily can we help you as well as helping that task which we have before us."

The young man shook his head in negation, and said, "No, the agreement was that I wanted to leave my body, you wanted to stuff someone else in it, that's all the agreement was, I hold you to it."

Suddenly there was a flash and the young man disappeared. My guide exclaimed, "Oh dear, dear, with such truculent thoughts, he could not stay with us here on this astral plane. Now we shall have to go to where he is sleeping in a room alone."

Together we on and upwards, but not into the astral world we had just been. This time we soared across the world to a house in England. We saw in the physical the face of the man whom I had previously seen only in the astral. He looked so discontented, so unhappy. We tried to attract his attention but he was sleeping very soundly indeed.

The lama whispered, "Are you coming?" I whispered, "Are you coming?" And we kept it up, first one and then the other, until at last very, very reluctantly the astral form of this man emerged from his physical body.

Slowly it oozed out, slowly it coalesced above him in the exact shape of his body, then it reversed its position, head of the astral body to the feet. The form tilted and landed on his feet. He certainly looked very truculent and, I could see, he had absolutely no recollection of seeing us before. This was astounding to me, but my companion whispered that he had been in such a bad temper and had slammed back in his body so violently that he had completely obliterated all memories of what had happened to him.

"So you want to leave your body?" I asked. "I most certainly do," he almost snarled back at me. "I absolutely hate it here." I looked at him and I shuddered with apprehension and, not to put too fine a point upon it, with pure fright. How was I going to take over the body of a man like this? Such a truculent man, so

72

My Visit To Agharta

difficult. But, there it was. He laughed and said, "So YOU want my body? Well, it doesn't matter what you want, it doesn't matter who you are in England, all that matters is who do you know, how much have you got."

We talked to him for a time and he grew calmer and I said, "Well, one thing, you will have to grow a beard. I cannot shave my beard because my jaws have been damaged by the Japanese. Can you grow a beard?" "Yes, sir," he replied, "I can and I will."

I thought for a moment and then I said, "Very well, you should be able to grow a suitable beard in a month. In one month's time, then, I will come and I will take over your body and you shall be allowed to go to an astral world so that you may recover your tranquility and know that there is joy in living."

Then I said, "It would help us greatly, greatly, if you would tell us your life story because although we have seen much in the astral by way of the Akashic Records there still is a boon to be derived by hearing the actual experiences from the person concerned."

He looked dreadfully truculent again, and said, "No, no I cannot bear to speak of it, I am not going to say another word."

Sadly we turned away and went into the astral world so that we could again consult the Akashic Record, to see much of his life, but in the Akashic Record one sees all that has happened, one does not necessarily get the unspoken opinions of a person, we see the act but not the thought which preceded the act.

But let us now take a leap forward from those days many years ago. The young man now, many years in the astral world, has mellowed somewhat, and to some small extent appreciates the difficulties with which we are confronted. He has, then, agreed to tell us his own life story. He upon the astral world, and I, Lobsang Rampa, here upon the world of Earth – trying to write down precisely as dictated those things which the young man tells. Here is a small part of his life story.

"All right for you – I thought – you haven't any trouble like I have. Here I am in this terrible world where I grew up poor and alone with no escape but death. When I grew up it was nothing but hardship. I had an awful job. I could never get a raise and my boss seems to have a dislike to me, why should I stay here? There are plenty of trees about and a nice rope to throw around my neck.

"But I am not saying too much about this, because a thought was put in my mind saying that if I wanted to, I could get release from what I considered to be the tortures of Earth. If I wanted to, if I was really serious, I could do something for mankind by making my body available to some ghost or spirit – which wanted to hop in almost before I had hopped out. It seemed a lot of rubbish to me, but I thought I would give it a whirl and let them talk on. First, they said, as a sign of genuine interest, I had to change my name. They told me a strange name they wanted me to adopt, so I told my wife only that I was going to change my name, she thought I was a bit mad or something and let it go at that, and so I did change my name quite legally.

"Then one night I was approached by a group of men. They grabbed me out of my body, and talked to me, and they asked me if I still wanted to get out of my body, into what I then thought was Paradise. I suppose it is Paradise, but these people called it the astral world. I assured them I wanted to get out even more than before, so they told me that the very next day I must stay at home. One man, he was all done up in a yellow robe, took me to the window and pointed out. He said, "That tree – you must go to that tree and put your hands up on that branch, and go to pull yourself up and then let go." He gave me the exact time at which I must do this, telling me it was utterly vital to follow instructions to the letter, otherwise I would have a lot of pain, and so would other people. But worse, for me, I would still be left on the Earth.

"The next day my wife thought I had gone bonkers or something because I didn't go out as usual, I pottered about. And then a minute or two before the appointed time I went out into the garden and walked over to the tree. I pulled on a branch of ivy, or whatever it is that ivy has, and reached up to the branch as directed. And then I felt as if I had been struck by lightning. I had no need to pretend to fall, I did fall – whack down! I fell down, and then, good gracious me, I saw a silver rope sticking out of me. I went to grab it to see what it was but gently my hands were held away.

"I lay there on the ground feeling horribly frightened, because two people were at that silver rope, and they were doing something to it, and a third person was there with another silver rope in his hand, and, horror of horrors, I could see through the whole bunch of them, so I wondered if I was seeing all this, or if I had dashed my brains out, it was all so strange.

"At last there was a sucking sort of noise and a plop, and then I found – oh joy of joy – I was floating free in a beautiful, beautiful world. That is all I am going to say about my unhappy past life. Now I am going back to my own part of the astral world. . ."

BECOMING A NEW PERSON

I am T. Lobsang Rampa, and I have finished transcribing that which was so unwillingly, so ungraciously told to me by the person whose body I took over...let me continue where he left off.

His body was upon the ground, twitching slightly, and I confess without too much shame, that I was twitching also, but my twitches were caused by fright. I didn't like the look of this body stretched out there in front of me, but a lama of Tibet follows orders, pleasant orders as well as unpleasant ones, so I stood by, while two of my brother lamas wrestled with the man's Silver Cord. They had to attach mine before his was quite disconnected. Fortunately the poor fellow was in an awful state of daze and so he was quiescent.

At last, after what seemed hours but actually was only about a fifth of a second, they got my Silver Cord attached and his detached. Quickly he was led away, and I looked at that body to which I was now attached and shuddered. But then, obeying orders, I let my astral form sink down on that body which was going to be mine. Ooh, the first contact was terrible, cold, slimy. I shot off in the air again in fright. Two lamas came forward to steady me, and gradually I sank again.

Again I made contact, and I shivered with horror and repulsion. This truly was an incredible, a shocking experience, and one that I never want to undergo again.

I seemed to be too large, or the body seemed to be too small. I felt cramped, I felt I was being squeezed to death, and the smell! The difference! My old body was tattered and dying, but at least it had been my own body. Now I was stuck in this alien thing and I didn't like it a bit.

My Visit To Agharta

Somehow – and I cannot explain this – I fumbled about inside trying to get hold of the motor nerves of the brain. How did I make this confounded thing work? For a time I lay there just helpless, just as if I were paralyzed. The body would not work. I seemed to be fumbling like an inexperienced driver with a very intricate car. But at last with the help of my astral brothers I got control of myself. I managed to make the bodywork. Shakily I got to my feet, and nearly screamed with horror as I found that I was walking backwards instead of forwards. I teetered and fell again. It was indeed a horrendous experience. I was truly nauseated by this body and was in fear that I should not be able to manage it.

I lay upon my face on the ground and just could not move, then from the corner of an eye I saw two lamas standing by looking highly concerned at the difficulty I was having. I growled, "Well, you try it for yourself, see if you can make this abominable thing do what you tell it to do!"

Suddenly one of the lamas said, "Lobsang! Your fingers are twitching, now try with your feet." I did so, and found that there was an amazing difference between Eastern and Western bodies. I never would have thought such a thing possible, but then I remembered something I had heard while a ship's Engineer; for ships in Western waters the propeller should rotate in one direction, and for Eastern waters it should rotate in the opposite direction. It seems clear to me, I said to myself, that I've got to start out all over again. So I kept calm and let myself lift out of the body, and from the outside I looked at it carefully – and once again I squeezed myself uncomfortably into the slimy, cold thing which was a Western body.

With immense effort I tried to rise, but fell again, and then at last I managed to scramble somehow to my feet and pressed my back against that friendly tree.

There was a sudden clatter from the house and a door was flung open. A woman came running out saying, "Oh! What have you done now. Come in and lie down."

It gave me quite a shock. I thought of those two lamas with me and I was fearful that the woman might throw a fit at the sight of them, but obviously they were completely invisible to her, and that again was one of the surprising things of my life. I could always see these people who visited me from the astral, but if I talked to them and then some other person came in – well, the other person thought I was talking to myself and I didn't want to get the reputation of being off my head.

My Visit To Agharta

The woman came toward me and as she looked at me a very startled expression crossed her face. I really thought she was going to get hysterical but she controlled herself somehow and put an arm across my shoulders. Even though she never said anything at the time – she could sense that her husband was gone forever, to be replaced by some stranger.

Silently I thought of how to control the body and then very slowly, thinking a step at a time, I made my way into the house and went up the stairs, and flopped upon what was obviously my bed.

For three whole days I remained in that room pleading indisposition while I practiced how to make the body do what I wanted it to do, and trying to contain myself because this was truly the most frightening experience I had ever experienced in my life. I had put up with all manner of torments in China and in Tibet and in Japan, but this was a new and utterly revolting experience, the experience of being imprisoned in the body of another person and having to learn all over how to control it.

I thought of that which I had been taught so many years ago, so many years ago that indeed it seemed to be a different life. "Lobsang," I had been told, "in the days of long ago the Great Beings from far beyond this system and Beings who were not in human form, had to visit this Earth for special purposes. Now, if they came in their own guise they would attract too much attention, so always they had bodies ready which they could enter and control, and appear to be the natives of the place. In the days to come," I was told, "you will have such an experience, and you will find it to be utterly shocking."

I did!

THE LONG LOST BOOKS OF RAMPA
Section Three
You-Forever

You-Forever is a guide to understanding the psychic world and how to develop your paranormal abilities. Now - many years after this was written - a number of similar books about these themes has appeared, and in comparison, one can see the extreme accuracy of Rampa's descriptions regarding the aura, paranormal abilities, out of the body/astral trips, life on the other side, the reincarnation process, and so on. Rampa also describes how and what "life" is as seen both from the physical and the psychical side.

THE BRAIN AND THE OVERSELF

The brain generates electricity of its own!(on a chemical way). Within the human body there are traces of metals, even metals such as zinc, and of course we must remember that the human body has the carbon molecule as its basis. There is much water in a body, and traces of chemicals such as magnesium, potassium, etc. These combine to form an electric current, a minute one, but one which can be detected, measured, and chatted.

A person who is mentally ill can, by the use of a certain instrument, have his brain waves charted. Various electrodes are placed upon his head and little pens get to work on a strip of paper. As the patient thinks of certain things the pens draw four squiggly lines which can be interpreted to indicate the type of illness from which the patient is suffering. Instruments such as this are in common use in all mental hospitals. The brain is, of course, a form of receiving station for the messages which are transmitted by the Overself, and the human brain in its turn can transmit messages, such as lessons learned, experiences gained, etc., to the Overself. These messages are conveyed by means of the "Silver Cord," a mass of high velocity molecules, which vibrate and rotate at an extremely divergent range of frequencies, and connects the human body and the human Overself.

The body here on Earth is something like a vehicle operated by remote control. The driver is the Overself. You may have seen a child's toy car, which is connected, to the child by a long flexible cable. The child can press a button and make the car go forward, or make it stop or go back, and by turning a wheel on this flexible cable the car can be steered. The human body may be likened very, very roughly to that, for the Overself which cannot come down to the Earth to gain experience, sends down this body which is us on Earth.

Everything that we experience, everything that we do or think or hear – travels upwards to be stored in the memory of the Overself. Very highly intelligent men, who get "inspiration," often obtain a message consciously from the Overself by way of the Silver Cord. Leonardo da Vinci and Nikola Tesla were two who were constantly in touch with their Overselves. Great artists or great musicians are those in touch with their Overself on perhaps one or two particular "lines," and so they come back and compose "by inspiration" – music or paintings – which have been more or less dictated to them by the Greater Powers which control us.

This Silver Cord connects us to our Overself in much the same way as the umbilical cord connects a baby to its mother. The umbilical cord is a very intricate device, a very complex affair indeed, but it is as a piece of string compared to the complexity of the Silver Cord. This Cord is a mass of molecules rotating over an extremely wide range of frequencies, but it is an intangible thing – so far as the human body is concerned. The molecules are too widely dispersed for the average human sight to see it. Many animals can see it, because animals see on a different range of frequencies – and hear on a different range of frequencies than humans. Dogs, as you know, can be called by a "silent" dog whistle, silent because a human cannot hear it – but a dog easily can. In the same way, animals can see the Silver Cord and the aura, because both these vibrate on a frequency which is just within the receptivity of an animal's sight.

With practice it is quite easily possible for a human to extend the band of receptivity of their sight, in much the same way as a weak man, by practice and by exercise, can lift a weight which normally would be far beyond his physical capabilities. The Silver Cord is a mass of molecules, a mass of vibrations.

My Visit To Agharta

One can liken it to the tight beam of radio waves which scientists bounce off the Moon. Scientists trying to measure the distance of the Moon, broadcast on a very narrow beam - a waveform to the surface of the Moon. That is much the same as the Silver Cord between the human body and the human Overself; it is the method whereby the Overself communicates with the body on Earth.

Everything we do is known to the Overself. People strive to become spiritual if they are on "the right Path." Basically, in striving for spirituality, they strive to increase their own rate of vibration on Earth, and by way of the Silver Cord – to increase the rate of vibration of the Overself. The Overself sends down a part of itself into a human body in order that lessons may be learned and experiences gained. Every good deed we do, increases our Earth's – and our astral rate of vibration, but if we do an evil deed to some person, that decreases and subtracts from our rate of spiritual vibration. Thus, when we do an ill turn to another, we put ourselves at least one step down on the ladder of evolution, and every good deed we do increases our own personal vibration by a like amount.

Thus it is that it is so essential to adhere to the old Buddhist formula – which exhorts one to "return good for evil and to fear no man, and to fear no man's deed, for in returning good for evil, and giving good at all times, we progress upwards and never downwards."

Everyone knows of a person who is "a low sort of fellow." Some of our metaphysical knowledge leaks over into common usage – in much the same way as we say a person is in a "black mood," or a "blue mood." It is all a matter of vibration, all a matter of what the body transmits by way of the Silver Cord to the Overself, and what the Overself sends back again by way of the Silver Cord to the body.

Many people cannot understand their inability to consciously contact their Overself. It is quite a difficult matter without long training. Supposing you are in South America and you want to telephone someone in Russia, perhaps in Siberia. First of all you have to make sure that there is a telephone line available, then you have to take into consideration the difference in time between the two countries. Next you have to make sure that the person you want to telephone is available and can speak your language, and after all that you have to see if the authorities will permit of such a telephone message!

My Visit To Agharta

It is better at this stage of evolution, not to bother too much about trying to contact one's Overself consciously, because no course, no information, will give you in a few written pages – what it might take ten years of practice to accomplish. Most people expect too much; they expect that they can read a course and immediately go and do everything that the Masters can do, and the Masters may have studied a lifetime, and many lifetimes before that! Read this book, study it, ponder upon it, and if you will open your mind – you may be granted enlightenment. We have known many cases where people received certain information and they then could actually see the etheric or the aura or the Silver Cord. We have many such experiences to fortify us in our statement that you, too, can do this if you will permit yourself to believe!

It is easily possible for an Adept to look at a person and to actually see on the outer covering of the aura some of the things that the subject has done during the past two or three lives. It may sound fantastic to the uninitiated, but nevertheless it is perfectly correct.

Matter cannot be destroyed. Everything that is – still exists. If you make a sound the vibration of that sound – the energy which it causes – goes on forever. If, for instance, you could go from this Earth quite instantly to a far, far planet – you would see, provided you had suitable instruments – pictures which happened thousands and thousands of years before. Light has a definite speed, and light does not fade, so that if you got sufficiently distant from the Earth (instantly) – you would be able to see the creation of the Earth! But this is taking us away from the subject under discussion. We want to make the point that the subconscious, not being controlled by the conscious, can project pictures of things beyond the present reach of the conscious. And so a person with good powers of clairvoyance can easily see what manner of person faces him. This is an advanced form of psychometry, it is what one might term "visual psychometry."

Everyone with any perception or sensitivity at all, can sense an aura, even when they do not actually see it. How many times have you been instantly attracted, or instantly repelled by a person when you have not even spoken to him? Unconscious perception of the aura explains one's likes and dislikes. All peoples used to be able to see the aura, but through abuses of various kinds, they lost the power. During the next few centuries people are going once again to be able to do telepathy, clairvoyance, etc.

My Visit To Agharta

Let us go further into the matter of likes and dislikes: every aura is composed of many colours and many striations of colours. It is necessary that the colours and striations match each other before two people can be compatible. It is often the case that a husband and a wife will be very compatible in one or two ways, and completely incompatible in others. That is because the particular wave form of one aura only touches the wave form of the partner's aura at certain definite points and on those points there is complete agreement and complete compatibility. We say, for instance, that two people are poles apart, and that is definitely the case when they are incompatible. If you prefer, you can take it that people who are compatible have auric colours, which blend and harmonize – whereas those who are incompatible have auric colours, which clash and would be really painful to look upon.

People come of certain types. They are of common frequencies. People of a "common" type go about in a body. You may get a whole group of girls going about together, or a whole group of young men lounging on street corners or forming gangs. That is because all these people are of a common frequency or common types of aura, they depend upon each other, they have a magnetic attraction for each other, and the strongest person in the group will dominate the whole and influence them for good or for bad. Young people should be trained by discipline and by self, discipline to control their more elementary impulses, in order that the race as a whole may be improved.

As already stated, a human is centered within the egg – shape covering – centered within the aura, and that is the normal position for most people, the average, healthy person. When a person has a mental illness, he or she is not properly centered. Many people have said, "I feel out of myself today." That may well be the case, a person may be projecting at an angle inside the ovoid. People who are of dual personality are completely different from the average, they may have half the aura of one colour, and half of a completely different colour pattern.

They may – if their dual personality is marked – have an aura which is not just one egg-shaped aura, but has two eggs joined together at an angle to each other. Mental illness should not be treated so lightly. Shock treatment can be a very dangerous thing because it can drive the astral straight out of the body. But in the main shock treatment is designed (consciously or unconsciously!) to shock the two "eggs" into one. Often it just "burns out" neural patterns in the brain.

82

My Visit To Agharta

We are born with certain potentialities, certain limits as to the colouring of our auras, the frequency of our vibrations and other things, and it is thus possible for a determined, well – intentioned person to alter his or her aura for the better. Sadly, it is much easier to alter it for the worse! Socrates, to take one example, knew that he would be a good murderer, but he was not going to give in to the blows of fate and so he took steps to alter his path through life. Instead of becoming a murderer, Socrates became the wisest man of his age. All of us can, if we want to, raise our thoughts to a higher level and so help our auras. A person with a muddy coloured red in the aura, which shows excessive sexuality, can increase the rate of vibration of the red by sublimating the sexual desires and then he will become one with much constructive drive, one who makes his way through life.

The aura vanishes soon after death, but the etheric may continue for quite a long time, it depends on the state of health of its former possessor. The etheric can become the mindless ghost, which carries out senseless haunting's. Many people in the country districts have seen a form of bluish glow over the graves of those who have just been interred. This glow is particularly noticeable by night. This, of course, is merely the etheric dissipating away from the decomposing body.

In the aura low vibrations give dull muddy colours, colours which nauseate rather than attract. The higher one's vibrations become – the purer and the more brilliant become the colours of the aura, brilliant not in a garish way, but in the best, the most spiritual way. One can only say that pure colours are "delightful" while the muddy colours are distasteful. A good deed brightens one's out – look by brightening one's auric colours. A bad deed makes us feel "blue" or puts us in a "black" mood. Good deeds – helping others – make us see the world through "rose tinted spectacles."

It is necessary to keep constantly in mind that the colour is the main indicator of a person's potentialities. Colours change, of course, with one's moods, but the basic colours do not change unless the person improves (or deteriorates) the character. You may take it that the basic colours remain the same, but the transient colours fluctuate and vary according to the mood. When you are looking at the colours of a person's aura you should ask:

❏   **(1.) What is the colour?**

❑   **(2.) Is it clear or muddy, how plainly can I see through it?**

❑   **(3.) Does it swirl over certain areas, or is it located almost permanently over one spot?**

❑   **(4.) Is it a continuous band of colour holding its shape and its form, or does it fluctuate and have sharp peaks and deep valleys?**

❑   **(5.) We must also make sure that we are not prejudging a person because it is a very simple matter to look at an aura and imagine that we see a muddy colour when actually it is not muddy at all. It may be our own wrong thoughts and preconceptions which makes a colour appear muddy, remember, in looking at another persons aura we first have to look through our own aura!**

The human body, consisting of molecules with a certain amount of space between atoms, also houses other bodies, tenuous bodies, spirit bodies, or what we call astral bodies. These tenuous bodies are precisely the same as to composition as is the human body, that is, they consist of molecules. But just as earth or lead or wood consists of a certain arrangement of molecules, molecules of a certain density, spirit bodies have their molecules fewer and further between each. Thus it is quite possible for a spirit body to fit into a flesh body in the most intimate contact, and neither occupies space needed by the other.

The astral body and the physical body are connected together by the Silver Cord. This latter is a mass of molecules vibrating at a tremendous speed. It is in some ways similar to the umbilical cord, which connects a mother to her baby; in the mother-impulses, impressions, and nourishment flow from her to the unborn baby.

When the baby is born and the umbilical cord is severed, then the baby dies to the life it knew before, that is, it becomes a separate entity, a separate life, it is no longer a part of the mother, so it "dies" as part of the mother and takes on its own existence.

The Silver Cord connects the Overself and the human body, and impressions flash from on to the other during every minute of the flesh-body's existence.

My Visit To Agharta

Impressions, commands, lessons, and at times even spiritual nourishment come down from the Overself to the human body. When death takes place, the Silver Cord is severed and the human body is left like a discarded suit of clothes, while the spirit moves on.

This is not the place to go into the matter, but it should be stated that there are a number of "spirit bodies." We are dealing with the flesh – body and the astral body at present. In our present form of physical and spiritual evolution there are nine separate bodies, each connected to the other by a Silver Cord, but we are concerned now more with astral travelling and matters intimately connected with the astral plane.

Man, then, is a spirit briefly encased in a body of flesh and bones, encased in order that lessons may be learned and experiences undergone, experiences which could not be obtained by the spirit without the use of a body. Man, or the flesh – body of Man, is a vehicle which, is driven, or manipulated by the Overself. Some prefer to use the term "Soul," we use "Overself" because it is more convenient, the Soul is a different matter, actually, and goes to an even higher realm. The Overself is the controller, the driver of the body. The brain of the human is a relay station, a telephone exchange, a completely automated factory, if you like. It takes messages from the Overself, and converts the Overself's commands into chemical activity or physical activity, which keeps the vehicle alive, causes muscles to work, and causes certain mental processes. It also relays back to the Overself messages and impressions of experiences gained.

By escaping from the limitations of the body, like a driver temporarily leaving an automobile, Man can see the Greater World of the Spirit and can assess the lessons learned while encased in the flesh, but here we are discussing the physical and the astral with, perhaps, brief mentions of the Overself. We mention the astral in particular, because while in that body, Man can travel to distant places in the twinkling of an eye. Man can go anywhere at any time, and can even see what old friends or relations are doing. With practice, Man and Woman – can visit the cities of the world and the great libraries of the world. It is easy, with practice, to visit any library and to look at any book or any page of a book. Most people think they cannot leave the body because in the Western world they have been so conditioned for the whole of their life – to disbelieve in things which cannot be felt, torn to pieces and then – discussed in terms which mean nothing.

My Visit To Agharta

There are no limits to the knowledge of the Overself. There are very real limits to the abilities of the body – the physical body. Almost everyone on Earth leaves the body during sleep. When they awake, they say that they have had a dream, because here again, humans are taught to believe that this life on Earth is the only one that matters, they are taught that they do not go travelling around when asleep. So, wonderful experiences are rationalized into "dreams."

Many people who believe, can leave the body at will, and can travel far and fast, returning to the body hours later with a full and complete knowledge of all they have done, all they have seen, and all they have experienced. Nearly anyone can leave the body and do astral travelling, but they have to believe that they can do this, it is quite useless for a person to put out repelling thoughts of disbelief, or thoughts that they cannot do such a thing. Actually, it is remarkably easy to astral travel when one gets over the first hurdle of fear.

Fear is the great brake. Most people have to suppress the instinctive fear that to leave the body is to die. Some people are deathly afraid that if they leave the body they may not be able to get back, or that some other entity will enter the body. This is quite impossible, unless one "opens the gate" by fear. A person who does not fear, can have no harm whatever occur to him. The Silver Cord cannot be broken when one is astral travelling; no one can invade the body unless one gives a definite invitation by being terrified.

You can always – ALWAYS – return to your body, just the same as you always awaken after a night of sleep. The only thing to be afraid of is of being afraid; fear is the only thing which causes any danger. We all know that the things which we fear rarely happen!

Thought is the main drawback after fear, because thought, or reason, poses a real problem. These two, thought and reason, can stop one from climbing high mountains; reason tells us that a slip will cause us to be cast down and dashed to pieces. So thought and reason should be suppressed. Unfortunately they have bad names. Thought! Have you ever thought about thought? What is thought? Where do you think? Are you thinking from the top of your head? Or from the back of your head? Are you thinking in your eyebrows? Or in your ears? Do you stop thinking when you close your eyes? No! Your thought is wherever you concentrate; you think wherever you concentrate upon.

86

My Visit To Agharta

This simple, elementary fact can help you get out of your body and into the astral, it can help your astral body soar as free as the breeze. Think about it, think how thought has often kept you back – because you thought of obstacles, you thought of unnamed fears. Thought is where you concentrate, thought is within you only because you are thinking of yourself and because you think thought must be within you. Thought is where you want it to be, thought is where you direct it to be.

Man, when uncluttered by his own stupid fears and restrictions, could almost be a superman with greatly enhanced powers, both muscular and mental. Here is an example; a weakly, timid man steps off a sidewalk into a heavy stream of traffic. His thoughts are far, far away, perhaps on his business or upon what sort of a mood his wife is going to be in when he gets home that night. He may even be thinking of unpaid bills! A sudden hoot from an approaching car and the man – without thought – springs back into the sidewalk with a prodigious leap which would normally be quite impossible for even a trained athlete! If this man had been hampered by thought processes, he would have been too late, the car would have knocked him over. The lack of thought enabled the ever-watching Overself to galvanize the muscles with a shot of chemicals (such as adrenalin) – which made the subject leap far beyond his normal capability and indulge in a spurt of activity beyond the speed of conscious thought.

Mankind in the Western world has been taught that thought, reason "distinguishes Man from the animals." Uncontrolled thought keeps Man lower than many animals in astral travel! Almost anyone would agree that cats can see things that humans cannot. Most people have had some experience of animals looking at a ghost or becoming aware of incidents long before the human became so aware. Animals use a different system from "reason" and "thought." So can we!

First, though, we have to control our thoughts, we have to control all those weary tag ends of idle thought which constantly creep past our minds. Sit down somewhere where you are comfortable, where you can be completely relaxed, and where no one can disturb you. If you wish, extinguish the light – for light is a drawback in a case such as this. Sit idly for a few moments – just thinking about your thoughts, look at your thoughts, see how they keep creeping into your consciousness, each one clamoring for attention, that quarrel with a man at the office, the unpaid bills, the cost of living, the world situation, what you would like to say to your employer – sweep them all aside!

My Visit To Agharta

Imagine that you are sitting in a completely dark room at the top of a skyscraper; before you there is a large picture window covered by a black blind, a blind which has no pattern, nothing which could prove a distraction. Concentrate on that blind. First of all – make sure that there are no thoughts crossing your consciousness (which is that black blind), and if thoughts do tend to intrude, push them back over the edge. You can do so, it is merely a matter of practice. For some moments thoughts will try to flicker at the edge of that black blind, push them back, forcibly will them to go, then concentrate on the blind again, will yourself to lift it – so that you may look out at all that is beyond.

Again, as you gaze at that imaginary black blind, you will find that all manner of strange thoughts tend to intrude, they try to force their way into the focus of your attention. Push them back, push them back with a conscious effort, refuse to allow those thoughts to intrude (yes, we are aware that we have said this before, but we are trying to drive the point home). When you can hold an impression of complete blankness for a short time, you will find that there is a "snap" as if a piece of parchment is being torn, then you will be able to see away from this ordinary world of ours, and into a world of a different dimension – where time and distance have an entirely fresh meaning. By practicing this, by doing this, you will find that you are able to control your thoughts as do the Adepts and the Masters.

Try it, practice it, for if you want to be able to progress you must practice and practice until you can overcome idle thoughts.

LEARN TO USE YOUR ASTRAL BODY

Thought is where you want it to be. Outside of you, if you want it so. Let us have a little practice. Here again, you will need to be where you are quite alone, where there are no distractions. You are going to try to get yourself out of your body. You must be alone, you must be relaxed, and we suggest that for ease you lie down, preferably upon a bed. Make sure that no one can intrude and ruin your experiment. When you are settled, breathing slowly, thinking of this experiment, concentrate on a point six feet in front of you, close your eyes, concentrate, WILL yourself to think that you – the real you, the astral you – is watching your body from some six feet away. Think! Practice! Make yourself concentrate. Then, with practice, you will suddenly experience a slight, almost electric shock, and you will see your body lying with eyes closed – some six feet away.

88

My Visit To Agharta

At first it will be quite an effort to achieve this result. You may feel as if you are inside a big rubber balloon, pushing, pushing. You push and push and strain, and nothing seems to happen. It almost seems to happen. Then at last, suddenly, you burst through, and there is a slight snapping sensation almost as, in fact, puncturing a child's toy balloon. Do not be alarmed, do not give way to fright, because if you remain free from fright you will go on and on, and – not have any trouble whatever in the future, but if you are afraid you will go back into the physical body and will then have to start all over again at some other date. If you bounce back into your body there is no point in trying anything more that day for you will rarely succeed. You will need sleep first.

Let us go further, let us imagine that you have got out of your body with this simple easy method, let us imagine that you are standing there looking at your physical component and wondering what to do next. Do not bother to look at your physical body for the moment, you will see it again quite often! Instead try this: Let yourself float about the room like a lazily drifting soap bubble, for you do not even weigh as much as a soap bubble now! You cannot fall, you cannot hurt yourself. Let your physical body rest. You will, of course, have dealt with that before freeing your astral from this fleshly sheath. You will have made sure that your flesh-body was quite at ease. Unless you took this precaution, you may find when you return to it that you have a stiff arm or a cricked neck. Be certain that there are no rough edges that would press into a nerve, for if, for example, you have left your physical body so that an arm is extended over the edge of the mattress, there may be some pressure upon a nerve which will cause you "pins and needles" later. Once again, then, make sure that your body is absolutely at ease before making any attempt to leave it for the astral body.

Now let yourself drift, let yourself float about the room, idly move round as if you were a soap bubble drifting on air currents. Explore the ceiling and the places where you could not normally see. Become accustomed to this elementary astral travel because until you are accustomed to floating about in a room – you cannot safely venture outside.

We are going to repeat astral travel directions under slightly different wording. You are lying flat on your back on a bed. You have made sure that every part of you is comfortable, there are no projections sticking into nerves, your legs are not even crossed, because if they were, at the point where they cross you might have a numbness after just because you will have interfered with the circulation of the blood. Rest calmly, contentedly, there are no disturbing influences, nor are you worried – think only of getting your astral body out of your physical body.

Relax and relax yet more. Imagine a ghostly shape corresponding roughly to your physical body, gently disengaging from the flesh body and floating upwards like a puffball on a light summer's breeze. Let it rise up, keep your eyes closed otherwise, for the first two or three times, you may be so startled that you will twitch, and that twitch may be violent enough to "reel in" the astral to its normal place within the body.

People frequently jerk in a peculiar manner just when they are falling asleep. All too often it is so violent that it brings one back to full wakefulness. This jerk is caused by a too rough separation of the astral body and the physical body, for, as we have already stated, nearly everyone does astral travelling by night even if so many people do not consciously remember their journeys. But back to our astral body again.

Think of your astral body gradually, easily separating from the physical body, and drifting upwards to about three, or perhaps four feet above the physical. There it rests above you swaying gently. You may have experienced a sensation of swaying just when you are failing asleep; that was the astral swaying. The body is floating above you, possibly swaying a little, and connected to you by the Silver Cord which goes from your umbilicus to the umbilicus of the astral body

Do not look too closely because we have already warned you that if you become startled and twitch – you will bring your body back and have to start all over again on some other occasion. Suppose you heed our warning, and do not twitch, then your astral body will remain floating above for some moments, take no action at all, hardly think, breathe shallowly for this is your first time out, remember, your first time consciously out – and you have to be careful.

If you are not afraid, if you do not twitch, the astral body will slowly float off, it will just drift away to the end or the side of the bed – where quite gently, without any shock whatsoever, it will gradually sink so that the feet touch, or almost touch the floor. Then, the process of making "a soft landing" over, your astral will be able to look at your physical and relay back what it sees.

My Visit To Agharta

THE LONG LOST BOOKS OF RAMPA
Section Four
Beyond The Tenth

In this section Rampa talks about the death process, the afterlife and the astral worlds. He also answers some questions about the mystery of UFOs and about religions, the future and the Earth's development through the cosmic ages.

First of all let us deal with a person who is leaving this Earth. The person is very, very sick usually, and 'death' follows as a result of the breakdown of the human body mechanism. The body becomes untenable, inoperable, it becomes a day case enshrouding the immortal spirit which cannot bear such restraint, so the immortal spirit leaves. When it has left the dead body, when it has left the familiar confines of the Earth, the, what shall we call it? Soul, Overself, Spirit, or what? Let's call it Soul this time for a change – the Soul, then, is in strange surroundings where there are many more senses and faculties than those weak, material senses experienced on Earth.

Here on Earth we have to clomp around, or sit in a tin box, which we call a car, but unless we are rich enough to pay airfares we are earthbound. Not so when we are out of the body, because when out of the body, when in this new dimension which we will call "the astral world," we can travel at will and instantly by thought, we do not have to wait for a bus or a train, we are not hampered by a car, nor by an aeroplane – where one waits longer in a waiting room than one spends on the actual journey.

In the astral we can travel at any speed we will. "We will" is a deliberate pair of words, because we actually *will* the speed at which wc travel, the height and the route. If, for example, you want to enjoy the wondrous scenery of the astral world with its verdant – and its lushly stocked lakes, we can drift as light as thistledown just above the land, just above the water, or we can rise higher and soar over the astral mountain tops.

91

My Visit To Agharta

When we are in this new and wonderful dimension, we are experiencing so many changes that unless we are very careful, we tend to forget those who mourn us on that awful old ball of Earth – which we have so recently left. We tend to forget, but if people on Earth mourn us too fervently, then we feel inexplicable twinges and pulls, and strange feelings of sorrow and sadness. Any of you who have neuritis or chronic toothache, will know what it's like; you get a sudden vicious jerk at a nerve which nearly lifts you out of the chair. In the same way, when we are in the astral world and a person is mourning us with deep lamentation, instead of getting on with their own affairs, they hinder us, they provide unwanted anchors which retard our progress.

Let us go just a little beyond our first days in the astral, let as go to the time when we have entered the Hall of Memories, when we have decided what work we are going to do in the astral, how we are going to help others, how we are going to learn ourselves. Let us imagine that we are busy at our task of helping or learning, and then just imagine a hand jerking at the back of our neck – tweak, tweak, tweak, and pull, pull, pull – it distracts the attention, it makes learning hard, it makes helping others very difficult, because we cannot add our full concentration or attention to that which we should be doing – because of the insistent tug and interference caused by those mourning us upon the Earth.

Many people seem to think that they can get in touch with those who have passed over by going to a back street medium, paying a few dollars or a, few shillings and just getting a message like having a telephone answered by an intermediary. Well, even this telephone business; try telephoning Spain from Canada! Try telephoning England from Uruguay! First you have the difficulty that the intermediary, that is the telephone operator on Earth, or the medium, is not familiar with the circumstances, may even be not very familiar with the language in which we desire to speak. And then there are all sorts of hisses, clicks, and clunks on the wire, reception may be difficult, reception, in fact, is often impossible.

Yet here on Earth we know the telephone number we desire to call, but who is going to tell you the telephone number of a person who recently left the Earth and now lives in the astral world? A telephone number in the astral world? Well, near enough, because every person on every world has a personal frequency, a personal wavelength. In just the same way as the BBC radio stations, or the Voice of America stations in the USA have their own frequencies, people also have

92

frequencies, and if we know those frequencies, we can tune-in to the radio station, provided atmospheric conditions are suitable, the time of the day is correct, and the station is actually broadcasting. It is not possible to tune-in and be infallibly sure that you can receive a station – for the simple reason that something may have put them out of action.

It is the same with people who have passed beyond this life. You may be able to get in touch with them if you know their basic personal frequency, and if they are able to receive a telepathic message on that frequency. For the most part, unless a medium is very, very experienced indeed, he or she can be led astray by some nuisance-entities who are playing at being humans and who can pick up the thoughts of what the caller wants.

That is, supposing Mrs. Brown, a new widow, wants to get in touch with Mr. Brown, a newly freed human who has escaped to the Other Side, one of these lesser entities who are not humans can perceive what she wants to ask Mr. Brown, can perceive from Mrs. Brown's thoughts how Mr. Brown spoke, what he looked like.

So the entity, like a naughty schoolboy who didn't get the discipline that he sadly needed, can influence the well-meaning medium by giving her a description of Mr. Brown which has just been obtained from the mind of Mrs. Brown. The medium will give "startling proof" by describing in detail the appearance of Mr. Brown who is "standing by me now." Well, the very experienced person cannot be deceived in that way, but the very experienced person is few and far between, and just does not have time to deal with such things. Furthermore, when commerce comes into it, when a person demands such-and-such a sum for a mediumistic sitting, a lower vibration is brought into the proceedings and a genuine message is thus all too frequently prevented.

It is unkind and unfair to let your sorrows harm and handicap a person who has left the Earth and who is now working elsewhere. After all, supposing you were very busy at some important task, and supposing some other person whom you could not see – kept jerking at the nape of your neck and prodding you, and blaring silly thoughts into your ears, your concentration would go and you really would call down all sorts of unkind thoughts upon your tormentor. Be sure that if you really love the person who has left the Earth, and if that person really loves you, you will meet again – because you will be attracted together when you also leave the Earth.

My Visit To Agharta

In the astral world you cannot meet a person whom you hate or who hates you, it just cannot be done, because that would disrupt the harmony of the astral world and that cannot be. Of course, if you are doing astral travel you can go to the lower astral which is, one might say, the waiting room or entrance to the real astral world. In the lower astral one can discuss differences with some heat, but in the higher regions – no.

So remember this: if you really love the other person and the other person really loves you, you will be together again – but on a very different footing. There will be none of the misunderstandings as upon this Earth, one cannot tell lies in the astral world, because in that world everyone can see the aura, and if an astral-dweller tells a lie, then anyone in sight knows about it immediately, because of the discord which appears in his personal vibrations and in the colours of the aura. So one learns to be truthful.

People seem to have the idea that unless they have a lavish funeral for the departed and go into ecstasies of sorrow, they are not showing a proper appreciation of the deceased. But that is not the case; mourning is selfish, mourning causes grave interference and disturbance to the person newly arrived in the astral plane. Mourning, in fact, could really be regarded as self-pity, sorrow for oneself that one has lost a person who did so much for those left behind. It is better and shows greater respect and thought – to control grief and avoid hysterical outbursts, which cause such distracts to people who have really left.

THE REALITY OF THE ASTRAL WORLDS

The astral worlds (yes, definitely plural!) are very real. Things are as real and as substantial upon those worlds as they appear to us to be here on this Earth, actually they appear more substantial, because there are extra senses, extra abilities, extra colours, and extra sounds. We can do so much more in the astral state.

There is not just one astral world, but many, as many in fact as there are different vibrations of people. Perhaps the best way of realizing this is by considering radio; in radio there are many, many different radio stations in all parts of the world. If those stations tried to share a common wavelength or frequency, there would be bedlam, everyone would interfere with everyone else, and so radio stations each have their own separate frequency, and if you want the BBC, London, you tune-in to those frequencies allotted to the BBC. If you want Moscow – you tune-in to the frequencies allotted to Moscow. There are thousands of different radio stations, each with their own frequency, each a separate entity not interfering with the others.

In the same way astral worlds are different planes of existence having different frequencies, so that upon astral world X, for example, you will get all people who are compatible within certain limits. In astral world *Y* you will find another set of people who are compatible within their own limits. Lower down, in what we call the lower astral, there are conditions somewhat the same as on the Earth, that is there are mixed types of people, and the average person who gets out of his body during the hours of sleep and goes astral travelling, he goes to that lower astral where all entities may mix. The lower astral, then, is a meeting place for people of different races and different creeds, and even from different worlds. It is very similar to life upon Earth.

As we progress higher we find the frequencies becoming purer and purer. Whereas in the lower astral you can have an argument with a person and tell him you hate the sight of him if you want to. When you get higher in the astral planes you cannot, because you cannot get people who are opposed to each other. So remember that the astral worlds are like radio stations with different frequencies, or – if you wish – like a big school with different classrooms, each succeeding class being higher in vibration than the one before, so that class or grade – *One* is a common denominator class, or astral world, where all may meet while the process of assessing their capacities goes on. Then as they do their allotted tasks, they become raised higher and higher until eventually they pass out of the astral planes altogether, and enter into a state where there is no longer rebirth, reincarnation, and where people now deal with much higher forms of being than humans.

But you want to know what happens when you die. It is very simple really. You leave your body and your astral form floats off and goes to the lower astral, where it recovers from shocks and harm caused by living or dying conditions on Earth. Then, after a few days according to Earth time reckoning, one sees all one's past in the Hall of Memories, sees what one has accomplished and what one has failed to accomplish, and by assessing the successes or failures – one can decide on what has to be learned in the future, that is, shall one reincarnate again right away, or shall one spend perhaps six hundred years in the astral. It all depends on what a person has to learn, it depends on one's purpose in the scale of evolution.

My Visit To Agharta

A very pleasant lady wrote to me and said, "I am so frightened. I am so frightened that I shall die alone with no one to help me, no one to direct me in the Path that I should take. You, in Tibet, had the Lamas who directed the consciousness of a dying person. I have no one and I am so frightened."

That is not correct, you know. No one is alone, no one has "no one." You may think you are alone, and quite possibly there is no one near your earthly body, yet in the astral there are very special helpers who await by the deathbed, so that just as soon as the astral form starts to separate from the dying physical body, the helpers are there to give every assistance. Just as in the case of a birth, there are people waiting to deliver the new-born baby. Death to Earth is birth into the astral world, and the necessary trained attendants are there to provide their specialized services, so there is no need for fear, there should never be fear. Remember that when the time comes, as it comes to all of us, for you to pass from this world of sorrows, there will be people on the Other Side waiting for you, caring for you, and helping you in precisely the same manner that there are people on Earth awaiting the birth of a new baby.

When the helpers have this astral body which has just been separated from the physical body, they treat it carefully and help it with a knowledge of where it is. Many people who have not been prepared think they are in Heaven or Hell. The helpers tell them exactly where they are, they help them to adjust, they show them the Hall of Memories, and they care for the newcomer as they, in their turn, have been cared for.

This matter of Hell – there is no such thing, you know. Hell was actually a place of judgement near Jerusalem, Hell was a small village near two very high rocks and between the rocks and extending for some distance around was a quaking bog which sent up blasts of sulphurous vapours, a bog that was always drenched in the stench of burning brimstone. In those far-off days a person who was accused of a crime was taken to this village and 'went through Hell.'

He was placed at one end of the bog and was told of the crimes of which he had been accused, he was told that if he could cross the bog unharmed – he was innocent, but if he failed and was swallowed by the bog he was guilty. Then the accused was goaded into action– perhaps a soldier poked him in a delicate part with a spear – anyway, the poor wretch ran "through Hell," through all the swirling fog

96

of sulphur and brimstone fumes, along the path surrounded by boiling pitch, where the earth quaked and shook, inspiring terror in the strongest, and if he reached the other side – he had passed through the valley of Hell and had been purged of any offence and was innocent again. So don't believe that you will go to Hell. You won't because there is no such thing.

God, no matter what we call Him, is a God of kindness, a God of compassion. No one is ever condemned, no one is ever sentenced to eternal damnation, there are no such things as devils who jump up and down on one and plunge pitch forks into one's shuddering body. That is all a figment in the imagination of crazed priests who tried to gain dominance over the bodies and souls of those who knew no better. There is only hope and knowledge – that if one works for it, one can atone for any crime, no matter how bad that crime seems to have been. So – no one is ever "extinguished," no one is ever abandoned by God.

Most people fear death because they have a murky conscience, and these priests who should know better, have taught about Hell – fire and eternal torment, eternal damnation and all that. And the poor wretched person who has heard those stories thinks that after he dies – he is going to be seized by devils and horrendous things done to him. Don't believe it, don't believe it at all. I remember all, and I can go to the astral at any time, and I repeat, there is no such thing as Hell, there is no such thing as eternal torment, there is always redemption, there is always another chance, there is always mercy, compassion, and understanding. Those who say that there is Hell and torment, well, they are not right in the head, they are sadists or something, and they are not worthy of another thought.

We fear to die for that reason and for another; we fear to die because the fear is planted in us. If people remembered the glories of the astral world – they would want to go there in droves, they wouldn't want to stay on this Earth any longer, they would want to shirk their classes, they would want to commit suicide, and suicide is a very bad thing, you know, it hurts oneself. It doesn't hurt anyone else, but one becomes one of life's drop-out's when one commits suicide.

Think of it like this; if you are training to be a professional person, say a lawyer or a doctor, well, you have to study and you have to pass examinations, but if you lose heart half way through – you drop out of your course and then you do not become a lawyer or a doctor, and before you can become a lawyer or a doctor you have to cease being a drop-out and get back into the class and study all over again. And by that time you find the curriculum has changed, there are different textbooks, and all you have learnt before becomes useless, so you start at the bottom again. Thus it is, that if you commit suicide, well, you have to come back, you reincarnate again, which is just the same as entering college for another course, but you reincarnate again and you learn all the lessons all over again right from the start, and all you learnt before is now obsolete, so you've wasted a lifetime, haven't you? Don't commit suicide, it's never, never, never worth it.

Well, that has taken us quite away from what people do in the astral. A lot depends on the state of evolution of the person; a lot of it depends on what that person is preparing for. But the astral worlds are very, very beautiful places, there is wonderful scenery with colours not even dreamed of upon the Earth, there is music, a music not even dreamed of upon the Earth, there are houses, but each person can build his or her house by thought. (But they are therefor not only "castles in the air," but solid and compact enough for the inhabitants of that frequency-world.

You think it, and if you think hard enough, it Is. In the same way, when you get to the astral world − first you are quite naked just as you are when you come to the Earth, and then you think what sort of clothes you are going to wear; you don't have to wear clothes, but most people do for some strange reason, and one can see the most remarkable collection of garments, because each person makes their own clothes according to any style they are thinking about. In the same way, they build their houses in any style they are thinking about. There are no cars, of course, and no buses, and no trains, you don't need them. Why be cluttered by a car when you can move as fast as you wish by wishing? So, by thought power alone, you can visit any part of the astral world.

In the astral there are many jobs that one can do. You can be a helper to those who are every second arriving from the Earth, you can do nursing, you can do healing, because many of those who arrive from the Earth are not aware of the reality of the astral, and they believe whatever their religion has taught them to believe. Or, if they are atheists − they believe in nothing, and so they are enshrouded in a black, black fog, a fog that is sticky and confusing, and until they can acquire some sort of understanding, that they are blinded by their own folly they cannot be helped much, so attendants follow them around and try to break away the fog. Then there are those who counsel the astral people who have to return to Earth. Where do they want to go, what sort of parents do they want, what sort of family conditions, a rich family or a poor family?'What sort of conditions will enable them to do the tasks which they plan to do? It all looks so easy when in the astral world, but it is not always so easy when one is on the Earth, you know.

In the lower astral people often eat, they can smoke also if they want to! Whatever they want to eat is actually manufactured from the atmosphere by thought, not so amazing when you think of prana which is believed in implicitly on Earth. So you can eat what you wish, you can drink what you wish also, but actually all that is just folly because one is acquiring all the energy, all the sustenance from the atmospheric radiation's, and eating and drinking is just a habit. One soon shucks off those habits and is the better for it. You can take it, then, that one does much the same in the lower astral as one does upon the Earth.

Yes, there is a sex life in the astral as well, but it is far, far better than anything you can ever experience on the Earth, because you have such an enhanced range of sensations. So if you have not had much of a balanced sex life on Earth, remember that in the astral you will have, because it is necessary to make a balanced person. Of course the higher one rises in the astral worlds, that is the more one increases one's personal vibrations, then the better the experiences, the more pleasant they become, and the more satisfying the whole existence becomes.

Many people on Earth are all members of a group. You may have, for example (and for example only) ten people whom together really complete one astral entity. On the Earth we have these ten people, and perhaps three, four, five, or six die; well, the person who is in the astral does not become really complete until all the group are united. It is very difficult explaining such a thing because it involves different dimensions, which are not even known upon this Earth, but you have felt a remarkable affinity with a certain person – a person who, of course, is absolutely separate from you.

You may have thought how compatible you were with that person, you may feel a sense of loss when that person goes away. Well, quite possibly that person is a member of your group, and when you die to this Earth, you will be united together as one entity. Upon the Earth all these people are like tentacles reaching out to get different sensations, different experiences during that brief flickering of consciousness which comprises a lifetime upon Earth. Yet – when all the members of that group, when all the tentacles are pulled in, one has in effect the experience of perhaps ten lifetimes in one. One has to come to Earth to learn the hard material things because there are no such experiences in the astral world.

Not everyone is a member of a group, you know, but you probably know whole groups of people who just cannot manage without each other. It may be members of a big family, they are always dashing around to see how the others are doing, and even when they marry they still have to forsake their partners at times and rush back home – as if they are all going in like a lot of chickens under the old hen! Many people are individualists, not members of a group upon the Earth, they have come to do certain things alone, and they rise or fall by their own efforts on the Earth. The poor souls often have a very bad time indeed upon the Earth, and it doesn't necessarily mean that they have immense karmic debts because they get suffering, it means that they are doing special work and incurring good karma for a few lives to come.

Really experienced people can tell what other people have been in a past life, but don't believe the advertisement you read – where, for a small sum of money, you can have all your past incarnations told. Don't believe that for a moment, because most of these people who make such claims are fakes. If they demand money for such a service, then you can be sure that they are fakes – because the really trained person does not take money for these occult purposes as it lowers the personal vibrations.

One could say that this life and the astral life are represented in this manner. The coarse vibrations of sound would represent life on earth – but the finer and higher vibrations of sight would represent the astral. There are many senses available to us in the astral, which we do not even know about when in the physical. People write to me and they ask how is it possible for a fourth dimensional person to, well, as an illustration, drop a stone into one's living room. The answer to that is that in the third dimensional world of the flesh, we are only able to perceive in the dimensions of the flesh, and if there was an opening somewhere else, the flesh body's eyes would not be able to perceive it.

Let us assume that humans can only look down, or they, are two dimensional. So, as they can only look down they cannot see the ceiling above. But if a person outside the room can perceive that there is no ceiling there, then that person can easily toss a brick in to the person who cannot look up. That is rather a crude way of explaining it, but what really happens is that every room, or everything on Earth, has another opening, another aperture, which humans on Earth cannot perceive, because they lack the necessary organ with which to perceive that dimension. Yet a person who is in a fourth dimensional world can make use of that opening and pass things through it into what, to the third dimensional inhabitant, is a closed space. This type of "joke" is often played by lower entities who like to pose as poltergeists.

Even scientists now agree that the brain generates electricity. There are medical procedures in which brain-waves are charted. A special apparatus is placed on the head, and four squiggly lines indicate four different levels of thought. For some strange reason these four squiggly lines are given Greek names, which doesn't concern us at all. But the brain generates electricity, and the electricity varies according to what one is thinking, in much the same way as if when one is speaking into a microphone, the words generate a current which continuously varies in intensity according to what is being said. In a tape recorder, for example, one speaks and ones speech impresses minute magnetic currents on a specially prepared tape. Afterwards, when the tape is played back, one obtains a reproduction of the original speech. The human brain generates an electric current which other brains can pick up, in much the same way as the tape on a tape recorder picks up the minute impulses from voice vibrations, which are transferred to electric impulses.

When you think, you broadcast your thoughts. Most, people are immune to the noise of the thoughts of other people, and fortunately so because everyone is thinking something all the time, and unless people were immune to that continuous, non-stop, never-ending noise, one would go quite round the bend. By special training, or by a fluke of Nature, one can tune-in to thoughts, because, as our brains generate electricity, so they are able to receive electric impressions. It is a form of telepathy which keeps the body, in touch with the Overself, the telepathy in this instance being a very special ultra high frequency current going from the brain of the flesh body, by way of the Silver Cord, and on to the Overself.

It is necessary only to say that every brain acts as a radio transmitter and radio receiver, and if you knew how to switch on your receiver, you would be inundated with everybody else's thoughts. You can pick up the thoughts of those with whom you are compatible – far more easily than you can pick up the thoughts of those with whom you are not compatible. And a good exercise is to guess what a person whom you know well is going to say next. If you guess for some time, you will soon discover that your successes are far outstripping the laws of chance, and when you begin to realize that you are well on the way to telepathic communication with the person with whom you are compatible. Here again, it is a matter which needs practice and patience, and when you are telepathic, you will wish you were not, because life will be a constant babble, what with humans and animals all the time talking to each other.

A LOOK TOWARDS THE FUTURE

We need spiritual discipline. A religion is a useful thing for inculcating spiritual discipline provided the religious leaders are not fighting among themselves. At the present day religions fall down on the job, and so all the present Earth religions shall, before too long, pass away like shadows disappearing in the night, and a fresh religion shall come to this earth which shall help lift people out of the, darkness and the misery into which they have now sunk.

But the time is not yet. The Final Battle is not yet. First there is more suffering, more disturbances in this, the Age of Kali, disturbances caused by World War One in which women deserted their homes and their children and left those children to run wild on the streets. If you get a wonderfully kept orchard, an orchard on which great care and endless expense has been lavished, and you suddenly withdraw all care from that orchard – everything soon becomes third-rate. The fruit no longer has the bloom and the fullness of constant care, instead that fruit becomes wrinkled and bitter. People are getting like that. People are now of inferior stock, and soon there will have to be the leaving process again so that fresh blood is brought to the Earth.

But first there will be more suffering. First the whole world will be engulfed by a form of Communism. Not the Communism of China, where even clocks and cars are supposed to run by the illustrious thoughts of Chairman Mao Tse Tung, and where, apparently, if a person has some interior obstruction, he just thinks of old Mao Tse Tung, and there is such a disturbance that everything is – cleared away immediately! Communism as we know it now will disappear from the Soviet Union and its satellite countries. But a new form of Communism will arise from the countries who thought themselves immune from the poisons of Carl Marx. So frankly, Earth is in for a for a bad time. Everything is going to be engulfed in this form of Communism. Everyone will be, given a number – they might even lose their names and identities. We will also see religious fundamentalism sweeping the planet. This fundamentalism will strike especially the Christian and Muslim religions and they will battle each other in a sick attempt to wipe each other off the face of the earth. This isn't justice. This isn't fair. And it's this type of sub-human person who is ruling the Earth today and will bring the Earth down even lower and lower.

I can think of no greater abomination than someone who hurts and kills in the name of God. They are perverting that which is good and true in our lives. They like to think of themselves as above the law, that God has approved their unholy quest. But in actuality, they are lower than the worms that crawl in the mud.

Until, having unnecessarily touched rock bottom in this, the Age of Kali, the indomitable spirit existing in some people, will shudder with the shock and the shame of what has fallen upon the Earth, and the spirit will revolt and will take action which will enable Earth and the peoples of Earth to rise again. But it may be necessary for the peoples of space, the Gardeners of Earth, to come and give assistance.

This is the Age of Assassination. A great religious leader, Martin Luther King, was assassinated. He was a good man and had much to give to this Earth. As for the others, well, they were just political people and (I do not want to tread on anyone's toes!) history will prove that these were dwarfs raised to giant stature only by the appalling power of their advertising machine – an advertising machine which blew out a lot of stinking hot air and made the dwarfs appear like giants, just as you can get a toy soldier, and by placing a light behind him, you can make his shadow giant size on the wall behind. But here, too, the toy soldier's shadow is a shadow only, something without substance, something that soon will be forgotten.

Martin Luther King was no shadow. He was a good man, working for the good, not only of people of colour, but of people of all colours throughout the world. For, in persecuting blacks, or browns, or reds or yellows, the white people who are doing the persecuting are placing a terrible amount of Karma upon themselves individually and collectively.

My Visit To Agharta

WHAT ARE UFOs?

High in the sky, beyond the height at aircraft would fly, there hovered a large silver pear shaped object, with the larger part pointing down and the smaller part pointing up. It hovered huge and in some alien way, menacing. "That's not a balloon!" said one man who had recently return from the Air Force. "If it was a balloon the larger would be at the top instead of at the, bottom."

"Yes," exclaimed another. "And it would be drifting with the wind. Look at those high alto-stratus clouds passing by it, and yet it is stationary."

The little town buzzed with consternation and speculation. High above, unmoving, inscrutable, hovered the enigmatic object. Never varying in position, making no motion, no movement of any kind. Slowly the day came to a close with the object there as though glued to a picture of the heavens itself, there unmoving, unchanging. The moon came up and shone across the countryside, and above in the moonlight the object loitered. With the first early dawn it was still there. People who were preparing to go to work looked out of their windows. The object was still there as if a fixture, and then, suddenly, it moved. Faster and faster it went, straight up, straight up into space, and disappeared.

Yes, you know, there are people in space ships who are watching this world. Watching to see what happens. "Well, why do they not come and talk to us like sensible people would?" you may ask, but the only reply is that they are being sensible. Humans try to shoot them, and a in any way to harm these UFOs.

If the UFOs, or rather the people within them, the intelligence to cross space, then they have the intelligence to make apparatus which can listen to earth radio and Earth television, and if they watch television – well, then they will think they have come to some vast mental home, because what could be more insane than the television programmes which foisted on a suffering public? Television programmes which glorify the unclean, which glorify the criminal, which teach sex in the wrong way, in the worst possible way, which teach people that only self-gain and sex matters.

Would you dive into a fish tank that you could discuss things with some worms at the bottom of the tank? Or would You go to a colony of ants – labouring in one

104

My Visit To Agharta

of these glass tanks designed to show the work of the ants? Would you go in there and talk with ants, or with any of these lesser creatures? Would you go into some glass hothouse and talk to some experimental plants, ask them how they are doing, saying: "Take me to your leader?" No!! You would watch, and if an ant bit you you'd say, "Spiteful little things, aren't they?" And be careful that you didn't get bitten in the future. So the people of space, whose one-year-old children would know more than the wisest man on this Earth, just watch over this colony.

A very few years ago I lived in Montevideo, the capital of Uruguay, a country which in South America lies between Argentina and Brazil. Montevideo is upon the River Plate and ships of the world pass by going to Rio de Janeiro or to Buenos Aires, or come into the Port of Montevideo. From my ninth a floor apartment I could look out across the River, right out to the South Atlantic – beyond the confines of the River. There were no obstacles, no obstructions, to the view.

Night after night my family and I used to watch UFOs coming from the direction of the South Pole straight over our apartment building, and coming lower so that they could alight in the Matto Grosso of Brasilia. Night after night, with unvarying regularity, these UFOs came. They were seen not just by us, but by a multitude of people, and in Argentina they are officially recognized as Unknown Flying Objects. The Argentine Government are well aware that these things are not the product of hysteria or a fevered imagination, they are aware that UFOs are real.

The day we landed in Buenos Aires – a UFO came in and actually alighted at the main airport. It stayed for several minutes at the end of a runway and then took off at fantastic speed. I was about to say that all this can be read in the press reports, but that is no proof of the truth of it – because too often the press alter things to suit themselves or to get more readers, and I have no faith whatever in anything which is printed in the daily press so, instead, I will say that this UFO landing is the subject of an Argentinian Government Report.

Having seen these UFOs night after night, and seen how they can change course and manoeuver, I state emphatically that these were not satellites flashing across the sky. The times that satellites can be seen varies, and is known to the minute; the times that we saw these other things were different, and in addition we have also seen the satellites. The night sky of Montevideo is remarkably clear, and I had a very high-power telescope which ranged from 40 magnification up to 350.

My Visit To Agharta

This world is under observation, but we need not be upset by that. It is sad indeed that so many people always fear that those who observe wish to do harm. They do not, they wish to do good. Remember that there are ages and ages going back into history, and various civilisations and cultures have appeared and disappeared almost without trace. Remember the civilisation of Sumeria, and the great civilisation of Minoa. Who has been able to explain the enigmatic statues of Easter Island? Yes, someone once tried to and wrote a sort of a book about it, but it's not necessarily accurate, you know. Or, if you want to go to another stage, how about the Maya people? Can anyone say what happened to the Mayan civilisation. Each of these civilisations was a fresh culture – placed upon the Earth to liven up stock which had become, dull and, what I can only term, 'denatured.'

There is also a very, very ancient theory, or legend, countless years ago a space ship came to this earth and something went wrong with the ship, it could not take off. So – the people aboard, men, women, and children, were marooned here, and they started another form of civilisation.

It is extremely fortunate that, the Hebrew Books of the Old Testament had been translated into Greek long before Christians came upon the scene, because the early Christians, just like the present day ones, tried to alter things to their own gain. We can, then, find out a lot about ancient history from the Hebrew Books which have not been tampered with by Christianity, but even they leave us uninformed about the Mayas, the Easter Islands, and the Etruscans.

These were civilisations which flourished more than 3000 years B.C. We can know that because Egyptian hieroglyphs can be traced back to the year 3000 B.C., and some of these, traced upon temple walls and in tombs, give information about earlier and very great civilisations. Unfortunately around about two hundred years after the start of Christianity, knowledge of much of this had been lost because of the manner in which Christians altered history to suit themselves, and because, with the rise in power of Christianity, Egyptian temples were closed down and no longer were there educated priests who could understand the hieroglyphs. And so for several hundred years history remained in darkness.

Later research indicates that many thousands of years ago a great Race suddenly appeared "in the Land of the Two Rivers." These people, now known to us as the Sumerians, have left little of their recorded history. Actually, according to the

My Visit To Agharta

Akashic Record, the Gardeners of the Earth decided that the "stock" on Earth was becoming weakened by inbreeding, and so they placed upon the Earth others who also had to learn. These others are known to us as the Sumerians, and a particular branch of the Sumerians – almost like a family – became the Semites, and they in their turn became the earliest Hebrews. But that was about 2ooo B.C.

The Kingdom of Sumeria was a truly mighty kingdom, and brought to this Earth many advancements in culture and science, and many different plants. Certain branch of the Sumerian culture left the founding city and moved to Mesopotamia in round about the year 4000 B.C. In addition they bred and gradually populated areas of high culture.

It is interesting to know that when Abraham moved with his herds from the City of Ur in Mesopotamia' and went to Palestine, he and those with him brought legends, which had been family history for thousands of years. They brought with them stories of the Garden of Eden, a land which lay between the Tigris and the Euphrates. This had been the common ground of many, many tribes and people who had been expanding – as their populations increased – over what is known as the Middle East. Eden, by the way, actually means "a plain." The Book of Genesis was merely a digest of stories and legends which had been told by the people of Mesopotamia for several thousand years.

Eventually civilisations became absorbed. So it was that the Sumerian civilisation, having leavened the stock of Earth, became absorbed and lost within the great mass of Earth people. And so, in different parts of the World and in different times, other "leavening cultures" had to be set down, such as the Etruscans, the Minoans, the Mayas, and the Easter Island people.

According to the old legends the Twelve Tribes of Israel do not altogether refer to the people of Earth, but instead mean one tribe which, was the original people of the Earth, and the eleven tribes, or cultures, which we're put down here to leaven the original which was becoming weakened by inbreeding.

Consider, for your own amusement, various tribes; the black people, the yellow people, the white people, and so on. Now which do you think is the original Earth inhabitant and which are descended from the Mayas – the Sumerians, the Etruscans, and others? It makes interesting speculation. But there is no need to speculate

107

because, I tell you vary seriously, that if you will practice what I have tried to show you in all my books, you can do astral travel. And if you can dd astral travel you can know what is happening, and what has happened, through the Akashic Record.

The Akashic Record is no television show where we are interrupted by a few words from our sponsor; here we have the utter truth, here we have absolute exactitude. History as it was, not as it was rewritten to suit some dictator who did not like the truth of his early life, for example.

By visiting the Hall of the Akashic Record you can find the truth about the Dead Sea Scrolls – those Scrolls which were found in 1947 in certain caves by the Dead Sea in a district called Qumran. This collection of scrolls belonged to a certain order of Jews who, in many ways, resembled Christians. They had a man at the head who was known as the Teacher of the Rightful Way. He was known as the Suffering Son of God, who was born to suffer and die for humanity. according to the scrolls He had been – tortured and crucified, but would rise again.

Now, you might think that this refers to the Leader of Christianity, Jesus. But this Teacher of the Rightful Way lived at least a hundred and fifty years before Jesus came to the Earth. The evidence is definite, the evidence is absolutely precise. The scrolls themselves were part of a library of this particular Jewish sect, and the library had been endangered by the Romans; and some of the Jewish monks had hidden certain Scrolls, probably the only ones that they had time to save.

There are various ways in which science can determine the age of any reputably antique object, and these scrolls have been subjected to those tests, and the tests indicate that they are about five hundred years older than Christianity. There is no possibility that they were written after the advent of Christianity. It follows from this that it would pay to have a really sound investigation into the Bible and all religious papers, because the Bible has been translated and re-translated many, many times, and even to the experts many of the things in the Bible cannot be explained. If only one could overcome religious bias, religious prejudice, and discuss things openly, one could get down to basic facts and the history of the world could be set right. There is, I repeat, a good way; and that is to consult the Akashic Record. Now, it is possible for you to do this if you first become proficient in astral travel.

My Visit To Agharta

The UFOs are merely the Gardeners of the Earth who come here from time to time to see, what is happening to their stock, and they have been here so much more frequently, and in much greater numbers recently – because mankind has, been playing around with atomic bombs, and risking blowing up the whole dump.

What a terrible commotion there has been about UFOs, hasn't there? Yet, UFOs are mentioned very extensively in the Greea Legends – and in the religious books of many different forms of religious belief. In the Bible UFOs are mentioned, and there are many reports in ancient monasteries, such as: "When the monks were sat down to lunch at midday – having their first meal of meat for many weeks, a strange aerial object came over and panicked the good, Brothers."

UFOs have been showing increasing activity during a past fifty or sixty years because the people of Earth have been showing increased hostility towards each other; think of WWII in which pilots of all nations saw what they called Foo Fighters, which were indisputably UFOs watching the progress of our battles. Then take the matter of airline pilots. It doesn't matter which airline, it doesn't matter which country, because airline pilots all over the world have seen many strange and even possibly frightening UFOs. They have talked about it extensively, too, but in many Western countries there is a heavy censorship about such things. Fortunate it is, too, or the press, with their usual distortions, would twist everything up and make the harmless into something horrendous.

It has usually been said, "Oh, well, if there are UFOs why have not astronomers seen them?" The answer is that astronomers have seen them, and have photographed them; but again there is such a censorship that people in prominent positions are afraid to talk about things they have seen. They are afraid to talk for fear of getting into trouble with the authorities who do not want the truth known. They are afraid to talk because, they fear that their professional integrity will seem to be in doubt, for people who have not seen UFOs are extremely virulent in their hatred for those who have.

So the pilots who fly the airlines, whether in a commercial capacity or in connection with the armed forces, have seen and will continue to see UFOs. But until the moronic governments of the world change their attitudes, not much will be heard of those sightings. The Argentine Government is surely one of the most enlightened in that they officially recognize the existence of UFOs. They were, in fact, the first country in the world to recognize UFOs as actualities. Other countries are afraid to permit any accurate information for various reasons. In the first case, the Christian belief seems to be that Man is made in the image of God, and, as nothing is greater than God – nothing can be greater than Man, who is made in the image of God. And so if there is some sort of creature who an make a space ship which can go through space, visiting different worlds, then that must be hushed up because the creature may not be in the shape of Man. It's all distorted reasoning, but things will change in the not too distant future.

Then the military clique cannot acknowledge the existence of UFOs because to do so would be to admit that there is something more powerful than the military clique. People also say that if there were UFOs the astronauts would have seen them. But that's not at all accurate, astronauts have seen UFOs and made statements to the press about their sightings. But again, censorship, both from governments and the media themselves, have kept most UFO reports by the astronauts away from the general public.

If you have listened-in to the astronauts radioing back to Earth you will have heard, or remembered that there have been references to these UFOs seen by astronauts, but in all future replays that reference has been carefully censored and deleted. The astronaut in the enthusiasm of the moment has mentioned UFOs. And also mentioned photographing UFOs, and yet in all later reports such references have been denied.

It seems; then, that we are up against quite a bad plot, a plot to conceal a knowledge of what circles Earth. A plot to conceal the very real existence of UFOs. In the press and in various pseudo-scientific journals there have been references to UFOs in the most scarey terms, how wicked these things are, dangerous, and how they do this or that. And I how have got a tremendous plot to take over Earth. Don't believe a word of it! If the UFO people had wanted to take over the Earth – they could have done it centuries ago. The whole point is, they are afraid that they will have to take over (and they do not want to), if the Earth goes on releasing too much hard atomic radiation out into space.

These spacemen are the Gardeners of the Earth. They are trying to save the Earth from us – and what a time they are having! There are reports of many different types of UFOs. Well of course there are! There are many different types of aircraft upon the Earth. You can, for example, have a glider without any engine. You can have a monoplane or a biplane; You can have a one-seater aircraft or a two-hundred-plus-seater aircraft, and if you don't want noisy aircraft then presumably you could get a spherical gas balloon or one of those very interesting things made by Goodyear. So, if you had a procession of these contraptions flying over darkest Africa, the people there would be most amazed at the variety, and would no doubt think that they came from different cultures. In the same way, because some spacecraft are round, or ellipse shaped, or cigar or dumb-bell shaped, the uninformed person they must come from different planets. Possible some of them do, but it doesn't matter in the slightest because they are not belligerent, they are not hostile. They are manned by quite benevolent people.

Most of these UFOs are of the same polarity as of the Earth, and so they can, if they wish, alight on the surface of the Earth and dive beneath the surface of the sea. But another type of UFO comes from the "negative" side and cannot come close to the Earth – perhaps I should say cannot come close to the Earth's surface – without disintegrating in a violent explosion with a tremendous clap of thunder, because these particular UFOs come from the world of antimatter. That is, the opposite type of world from this.

Everything, you know, has its equal and opposite. You can say that there is a sex thing in planets, one is male and the other is female, one is positive and the other is negative, one is matter and the other is anti-matter. So when you get reports of a tremendous explosion or see a vast fireball plunging to Earth and excavating a huge crater, you may guess that a UFO from an anti-matter world has come here and crashed.

There have been reports of so-called hostile acts by UFOs. People, we are told, have been kidnapped. But do we have any proof whatever that anyone has really been harmed? after all, if you have a Zoo and you want to examine a specimen, you pick up a specimen and bear it away. You examine it. You might test its blood, you may test its breath content – you could X-ray it and weigh it and measure it.

No doubt all those things would appear to be frightening and very tormenting to the ignorant animal involved. But the animal, when carefully replaced, is none the worse for this weighing and measuring, none the worse at all. In the same way, a gardener can examine a plant. He doesn't hurt the plant, he is not there to hurt

111

plants, he is there to make them grow – to make them better. So he examines the plant to see what can be done to improve it.

In the same way the Gardeners of the Earth occasionally pick up a specimen, a man or a woman. Well – so they measure a human, examine him or her – do a few tests, and then put the human back into the human surroundings. And he or she is none the worse off for it, it's only because they are scared silly that they think they are any the worse off. Usually they are so frightened that they concoct the most horrible tales about what happened to them, when, actually, nothing unusual whatever happened.

This world is being watched, and it has been watched since long, long before the dinosaurs thundered across the face of this Earth. The world is being watched, and it will be watched for quite a time, and eventually the people of space will come down here. Not as tormentors, not as slave-owners, but as benevolent teachers or guides.

Various countries now send what they call a Peace Corps to what are alleged to be under-developed countries. These Peace Corps people – who usually are in need of some form of excitement, or they can't get some other type of job – go out into jungles and teach "backward" people the things which they really do not need to know. Things which give them false ideas and false values. They get shown a film of perhaps some film stars marvelous palace in Hollywood and then they all get the idea that if they become Christians, or Peace Corps patrons, they also will have such a marvelous edifice in which to live, complete with swimming pool and naked dancing girls.

When the people from space come here – they will not behave like that. They will show people by example how they should go on, show them that wars are not necessary, show them a true religion which can be expressed in the words, "Do as you would be done by."

Before much longer, governments of the world will have to tell the truth about UFOs. They will have to tell about peoples from outer space. They know already, but they really are scared to let the public know. But sooner or later, they will have to let the public know, to adjust, to prepare, and to avoid any untoward incidents when our Gardeners return to this world.

My Visit To Agharta

People write to me about the so-called Men in Black. "Who are they?" I'm asked. The MIB are nothing more than outer space people here upon the Earth observing, recording, and scanning/planning. They are not here to cause trouble for anyone. They are here so that they may gain information with which they can best plan how to help the people of the Earth. Unfortunately too many Earth people are like mad animals, and if they think they are being attacked, they go berserk. If one of these Men (who may be dressed in any colour!) is attacked, then obviously he has to defend himself. But unfortunately his defense is often distorted to be an original attack when its nothing of the sort.

There are many types of UFOs. There are many shapes and sizes of people within those UFOs, but these people share one thing in common; they have lived a long time, longer than the people of Earth, and they have learned much. They have learned that warfare is childishness. They have learned that it is far better for people to get on together without all the quarreling. They have learned that Earth has apparently gone mad, and they want to do something to bring the people of Earth back to sanity. And if they cannot do that peacefully, then Earth will have to be – quarantined for centuries to come, and that would hold up the spiritual development of great masses of people here.

So do not fear UFOs for there is nothing to fear. Instead, open your mind to the knowledge that before too long, the people of this earth will have visitors from space who will not be belligerent but who will try to help us as we should help others.

PETS ON THE ASTRAL PLANE

I have been asked many times about our beloved pets and what happens to them when they pass onto the astral worlds. One lady in particular wrote me very upset because her minister had told her that the Bible says that only humans go to Heaven. The Bible was written a long time after the events related happened, the Bible is not the original Writings either. It is a translation of a translation of a translation of another translation, which had been re-translated to suit some king or some political power, or something else. Think of the King James Edition, or this Edition or that Edition. A lot of things written in the Bible are bunk. No doubt there was a lot of truth in the original Scriptures, but a lot of things in the Bible now are no more truth than the truth of the press, and anyone knows what a lot of bilge that is.

My Visit To Agharta

The Bible seems to teach humans that they are the Lords of Creation, that the whole world was made for Man. Well, Man has made an awful mess of the world, hasn't he? Where are there not wars, or rumours of wars, where is there no sadism, no terror, no persecution? You will have to move off this Earth if you want an answer to that. But we are dealing with animals and what happens to them.

In the first case there are many different species of creatures. Humans are animals, whether you like it or not humans are animals, horrid, uncouth, unfriendly animals, more savage than any of the Nature type animals.

Because humans have a thumb and fingers they have been able to develop along certain lines because they can use their hands to fabricate things, and that animals cannot do. Man lives in a very material world and only believes that which he can grasp between his fingers and his thumb. Animals, not having thumbs and not being able to grasp a thing in two hands, have had to evolve spiritually, and most animals are spiritual, they do not kill unless for the absolute necessity of eating, and if a cat terrorizes and tortures a mouse – well, that is an illusion of the humans; the mouse is quite oblivious of it because it is hypnotized and feels no pain.

Under stress a person's sensations are anaesthetized, so in times of war, for example, a man can have an arm shot off and apart from a very dim numbness, he will not feel it until loss of blood makes him weak. Or a person piloting a plane, for instance, can be shot through the shoulder but he will go on piloting his plane and bring it down safely and only when the excitement has ended will he feel pain. In the case of our mouse – by that time the mouse doesn't feel anything any more.

Horses do not reincarnate as daffodils. Marmosets do not reincarnate as maggots or vice versa. There are different groups of Nature people, each one in a separate isolated "shell" – which does not impinge upon the spiritual or astral existence of others. What that really means is that a monkey never reincarnates as a man, a man never reincarnates as a mouse although, admittedly, many men are mouse-like in their lack of intestinal fortitude which is a very polite way of explaining well, you know what.

It is a definite statement of fact that no animal reincarnates as a human. I know humans are animals as well, but I am using the commonly accepted term. One refers to humans and one refers to animals because humans like to be buttered up a bit,

114

My Visit To Agharta

and so one pretends that they are not animals but a special form of creature, one of God's chosen humans. So the human animal never, never reincarnates as a canine animal or feline animal, or equine animal: And, again, our old friend vice versa.

The human animal has one type of evolution which he must follow. Our animal friends has a different, and not necessarily parallel, form of evolution to follow. So they are not inter-changeable entities.

Many Buddhist Scriptures refer to humans coming back as spiders or tigers or something else, but of course that is not believed by the educated Buddhist, that started as a misunderstanding many centuries ago in much the same way as there is a misunderstanding about Father Christmas, or about little girls being made of sugar and spice and all things nice. You and I know that all little girls are not nice; some of them are very nice, some of them are proper stinkers, but, of course, you and I, we only know the nice ones, don't we?

When a human dies the human goes to the astral plane and when an animal dies it, too, goes to an astral plane where it is met by its own kind, where there is perfect understanding, where there is perfect rapport between them. As in the case of humans, animals cannot be bothered by those with whom they are incompatible, and now study this carefully; when a person who loves an animal dies and goes to the astral world, that person can be in contact with the loved animal, they can be together if there is absolute love between them. Further, if humans were more telepathic, if they were more believing, if they would open their minds and receive, then loved animals who had passed over could keep in touch with the humans even before the humans passed over.

Let me tell you something; I have a number of little people who have passed over, and I am still very definitely, very much in contact with them. There is one little Siamese cat, Cindy, with them. I am in daily contact, and Cindy has helped me enormously. On Earth she had a very bad time indeed. Now she is helping, helping, always helping. She is doing absolutely as much as anyone on the Other Side can do for anyone on this Side.

Those who truly love their so-called pets can be sure that when this life has ended for both, then they can come together again, but it's not the same. When humans are on the Earth, they are a disbelieving crew, cynical, hard, blasé and all the rest. When they get to the Other Side they get a shake or two which enables them to realize that they are not the Lords of Creation they thought they were, but just part of a Divine Plan.

On the other Side they realize that others have rights as well. When they get to the Other Side they find that they can talk with utmost clarity to animals who are also on the Other Side, and animals will answer them in any language they care to use. It is a limitation on humans that most of them while on Earth are not telepathic, most of them, while on Earth, are not aware of the character and ability and powers of so-called "animals." But when they pass over, it all comes clear to them, and when it comes to animals, humans then are like a person born blind who suddenly can see.

Yes, animals go to Heaven, not the Christian Heaven, of course, but that is no loss. Animals have a real Heaven, no angels with goose feathers for wings, it's a real Heaven, and they have a Manu, or God, who looks after them. Whatever Man can obtain or attain on the Other Side, so can an animal – peace, learning, advancement – anything and everything.

Upon the Earth man is in the position of being the dominant species, dominant because of the fearful weapons he has. Unarmed a man would be no match for a determined dog; armed with some artificial method such as a gun, a man can dominate a whole pack of dogs, and it is only through Man's viciousness that the telepathic power of communication with animals has been lost, that is the real story of the Tower of Babel, you know.

Mankind was telepathic for general use, and mankind used speech only in local dialects for communicating with members of the family when they did not want the community as a whole to know what was being said. But then Man lured animals into traps by false telepathy, by false promises. As a result mankind lost the telepathic power as a punishment, and now only a few people on this Earth are telepathic, and for those of us who are – it is like being a sighted person in the country of the blind.

Animals are not an inferior species. Humans can do a vast number of things that animals cannot, animals can do a vast number of things that humans cannot. They are different, and that's all there is to it – they are different, but not inferior. Now,

My Visit To Agharta

Miss Cleo my cat, resting so comfortably looked up with those limpid blue eyes and sent a telepathic message: "To work, we have to work or we do not eat." So saying she rose gracefully and most delicately walked off.

I have also been asked if there are any Mantras for sending dying animals to higher realms. One doesn't need Mantras from humans to animals; just as humans have their own helpers waiting on the Other Side of life to help the dying human to be reborn back into the astral, so animals have their own helpers. And so there are no Mantras necessary to help dying animals enter the astral world. Anyhow animals know by instinct, or by pre-knowledge, far more about such things than do humans.

One should not wait until an animal is dying before one is ready to help. The best way to help an animal is while it is alive and well on this Earth because animals are beautiful creatures, and there are no bad or vicious animals unless they have been made bad and vicious by the ill-treatment, conscious or otherwise, of humans. I have known many cats, and I have never known a cat who was naturally; vicious or bad tempered. If a cat has been tormented by humans, or by human children most likely, then of course it does adopt a protective fierceness, but soon with a little kind-ness all that goes, and one has a gentle, devoted animal again.

You know, a lot of people are scared stiff about Siamese cats, saying how fierce they are, how destructive, how everything bad. It isn't true, there isn't a word of truth in it not a word. Miss Cleopatra and Miss Tadalinka never, never do anything to annoy us. If something irritates us, then we just say, "Oh, don't do that, Clee!" and she doesn't do it again. Our cats do not tear up furniture or draperies because we have a pact with them; we provide a very easily made scratching post, actually we have two. They are sturdy posts, strongly mounted on a square base, both are covered with heavy carpet, not old scruffy carpet on which one has upset the garbage pail, but new carpet, actually off-cuts. Well, this carpeting has been securely fixed to the posts and on top of the posts there is room for a cat to sit.

Several times a day Cleopatra and Tadalinka go to their scratch posts, and they have such a long beautiful stretch that it makes one feel better just to watch. Sometimes they will walk up the post instead of jumping to the top, and that is very good for their muscles and very good for their claws. So, we provide the scratch posts and they provide the tranquillity because we do not have to fear for any furniture or any draperies.

My Visit To Agharta

Once I thought of writing a book about Cat Legends and the real story of cats. I'd love to, but increasing decrepitude makes it improbable that I ever shall. I would like to tell, for instance, how, on another world, in another system, far removed from the solar system, there was a high civilisation of cats. In those days they could use their "thumbs" as humans could, but, just as humans are doing now, they fell from grace and they had a choice of starting a round all over again or going to another system to help a race not yet born.

Cats are kind, creatures and understanding creatures, and so the whole race of cats and the Manu of cats decided to come to the planet we call Earth. They came to watch humans and report to other spheres on the behavior of humans, something like having a television camera watching all the time, but they watch and report not to harm humans, but to help them. In the better regions people do not report things to cause harm but only so that defects may be over-come.

Cats came to be naturally independent so they would not be swayed by affection. They came as small creatures so that humans could treat them kindly or treat them harshly, according to the nature of the humans.

Cats are benign, a good influence on Earth. Cats are a direct extension of a Great Overself of this world, a source of information where much information is distorted by world conditions.

Be friendly with cats, treat them kindly, have faith in them knowing that no cat has ever willingly harmed a human, but very many cats have died to help humans.

T. Lobsang Rampa with his cat Miss Cleo.

Photo courtesy The Rigberg Photo Collection

118

My Visit To Agharta

THE LONG LOST BOOKS OF RAMPA
Section Five
Candlelight

In *Candlelight* T. Lobsang Rampa uses his best endeavors to explain the Laws and the consequences of obeying or disregarding them. Rampa considers all life on earth to be a school and every living creature to be a pupil of that school; the disobedient ones will take longer to graduate than the pupils who want to learn and willingly accept knowledge.

BASIC TRUTHS, BASIC RULES

Far away, above all the trumpery laws and regulations of mankind, there are basic truths, basic rules which we transgress only at our peril. The laws of Man on Earth are not made for the individual but for the majority, and so that the best interests of a majority can be served often a law will appear to inflict hardship upon the individual. Never mind, that is one of the things we have to put up with if we are crazy enough to live in communities because liberty is a relative term.

If we were free to do anything at all, then we could go into anyone's house, take anything we wanted, do anything we wanted, and then we would be entirely free. Actually, that would not be to the benefit of the community as a whole and so there are laws to protect the majority against the minority, and we break those laws at our peril, peril on Earth, that is; most of them don't matter the slightest beyond this Earth. What does it matter, for instance, if a person buys a packet of cigarettes in England after eight o'clock in the evening? What does it matter if, in Canada, a person buys a newspaper on a Sunday? All these are childish stupid things, but somebody had an idea somewhere even if nobody knows what the sense of the said law now is!

No matter what kind or unkind things have been done to us by others – one consciously chooses the direction of his vision. Of course truth and justice or deceit and injustice can affect the course of our lives, either way towards – or away from the light, but isn't the application of the Golden Rule vitally important for each of us to practice, thereby helping others?

I say quite definitely that every person must stand alone. It is silly to join cults, gangs, associations, institutes, etc., etc., and to expect "salvation" thereby, because you won't find salvation in these money – making cults which are merely out to get your money! Look at it like this; a person dies – leaves this Earth for the astral realms – and that person is going to go to the Hall of Memories and answer to himself or herself for things which have been done or have not been done. There is no one else there except the newly arrived soul or entity or whatever you like to call it and the connection with the Overself. Now, I tell you quite definitely, quite, quite definitely, you answer alone. You won't get the secretary or chief tutor of the Hot Dog Society, or whatever you like to call all these cult things, to come and answer for you. You won't find the President of the Rednose Association coming and saying, "Oh yes, Overself, you don't know anything; I told this person to do such a thing because the rules of our Association say that it is so, so he should take your place."

You have to stand alone, then, naked and probably ashamed with it. And if you toss out all thoughts of these associations and cults on this Earth, then you will be in training to answer alone when you reach the Other Side.

Of course, if you are going to answer to your Overself then you need to have some good answers, and the best way is to obey the Golden Rule which is, Do unto others as you would have them do unto you. This person who writes this question seems to be wriggling and writhing and doing anything to evade the simple truth, the truth which is you have to learn to stand on your own two feet, no matter whether they are flat or not. You have to stand on them, you have to be responsible for yourself, and if you help others by adherence to and obedience of the Golden Rule, then you will have much good in your astral bank account.

Let me again state that God is not standing there with a whacking great cane, and the devil is not standing there with branding irons either. God is a positive force, the devil is a negative force, they are not people who praise or torture. While down here on this Earth you cannot understand things which happen in many more dimensions. In the same way a sea slug sitting on a bit of slime in the bottom of the ocean could not possibly understand what people on the moon are experiencing, it could not

My Visit To Agharta

at people in high – rise buildings are thinking or doing, nor
the commotion which is caused when people turn their
. All that would be completely beyond the comprehension of
ird dimension to try to understand what people in the ninth,
wentieth dimension are doing. So everything is relative. We
re or less what other people on Earth are doing, we might have
they are doing right or they are doing wrong, but how could
understand what twentieth dimension people are doing? You
he concepts of another dimension unless you have had some
mension.

get an idea, a rough idea, from thinking that everything is
call feel, a bit further we say sound, higher up still it is sight.
n, on any planet, on any system, or any universe, so that gives
tion of other dimensions. It is rare indeed for a person to feel
d, yet they are all vibrations, all part of the same scale. There
see sound, there are animals who can hear different sounds,
nd human range. Dogs, for instance, will respond to a whistle
lent to humans. Cats see colours on a different spectrum; cats,
as silver. But to give another slight illustration which might
his for yourself.

who was born blind. Now, you have the task of explaining to
born blind the difference between red and pink, or between
low are you going to do that? You can't. There is no way in
can explain to a blind person the difference between yellow
r and brown. You could possibly explain the difference
n if the person was extremely sensitive and could feel the
to know what other dimensions are like? Cut off a dimension
sight for example. Then how are you going to explain to a
known sight the difference between pink and red? It simply

Supposing you have a person who is completely deaf; how are you going to get that person to appreciate the difference between two fairly similar musical notes? Not so easy, eh? So unless you can give me answers to my questions I cannot tell you of the experiences of the ninth dimension.

My Visit To Agharta

ALL LIFE IS A SCHOOL

Let us consider life, all life is a school. Different classes, different grades. We on this Earth happen to be in Grade Three (third dimension). People in the fourth dimension are in Grade Four. People in the fifth dimension are in Grade Five. Now tell me seriously, thinking back to your own school days, can you truthfully say that the students in Grade Five at your school were very interested in staying on and helping the students in Grade Three? More likely the Grade Five, students thought the Grade Three students were crummy little punks who were beneath even a contemptuous notice. That is so, isn't it? So let me tell you this: there are certain people who are teachers who are unfortunate enough to be persuaded to volunteer to come to Grade Three to teach the crummy little punks in this class, and when they get down to Grade Three they find that the students are not at all anxious to learn (were you anxious to learn when you were at school?), so the teacher gets all sorts of nasty things said about him and eventually he gets really fed up with the whole procedure, and he says to the Headmaster, "Well Boss, I can't stick all these punks, I have to go to a different class or I shall go, even crazier. Where can you move me?"

So take it from me, the teachers on the Earth – teachers from other dimensions, are trying hard to do something to help the people in Grade Three, help the people in the third dimension. And if the people in the third dimension would be a bit more appreciative, they would get on much faster because there comes a time when even the best of teachers get sick and tired of continual persecution and wants to move on.

HOW TO DIRECT THOUGHT

We have to remember that we are only one/tenth conscious, and the real source of knowledge, the real source of action, is the subconscious. But the subconscious is like a lazy old man who wants to sit in front of the fireplace and smoke a pipe all day and not do anything. He knows he is the custodian of great knowledge, etc., but he doesn't want to part with any of it, he doesn't want to move. So you have to get through to him to somehow galvanize him into action. If you want to direct thought or control your mind, then you have to know what you want – because it is useless to seek a thing unless you know what you are seeking, otherwise you won't know when you have found it, will you?

My Visit To Agharta

Let us suppose you want to learn something; well, you sit down somewhere where it is quiet and you think of the matter which you desire to study. Perhaps you are afraid your memory will fail you or something, but anyway, you think of the matter you desire to study. Tell your subconscious what you want to do, tell your subconscious why you want to do it, say what benefits will be derived from learning such a matter.

You have to get it over to your subconscious that you and "George" or "Georgina" are all part of the same firm so what harms one – harms the other, what benefits one benefits the other. So you have to think about the thing you want to do, you have to think about it directly, you have to think all around it, you have to think of all the advantages. Then you have actually to visualize yourself studying the subject or possessing the object, and if you make a real campaign about it – do it perhaps three times in succession. The subconscious may be roused and will then help you to attain that which you desire.

You have to go in for visualization. Now, visualization is not imagination. Imagination is something which can be indulged in on the imaginary basis only. No amount of imagination, for instance, would enable you to jump over a thirty story building. You might be able to do it in your imagination and then you would be something like Buck Rogers, wouldn't you? But such a jump over a thirty story building is beyond the laws of physical nature so it is imagination only, and many people waste time imagining that which is impossible.

Visualization, on the contrary, is something, which is entirely possible, because it is entirely in keeping with normal physical laws. As an illustration, suppose you want to buy a boat, then if you visualize yourself suddenly coming into possession of a large sum of money and going to the place where they sell boats, looking over them, and finally deciding on such a boat – then you may find that your visualizations bear fruit. It is a fact that if the conditions are right, anything you visualize you can have in time. It may not be just at the moment you want it, or exactly as you had thought, but you will get it – if you visualize things properly.

You have to sit down comfortably. You have to cross your ankles and clasp your hands in front of you. Then you put out a very strong thought to your subconscious, calling him or her by the private name which I suggested earlier in this book. You tell your subconscious three times, "Attention! Attention! Attention!" Then you say,

"Look into my mind now." You repeat that three times, and then you think very definitely, very clearly on the matter for which you desire the cooperation of your subconscious.

USING THE PENDULUM TO DIRECT THOUGHT

We know, for example, that throughout countless years radium decays into lead. We know that all matter is a whole horde of molecules hopping about like fleas on a hot plate, the smaller the fleas the faster they can jump, the bigger the fleas, the slower and more cumbersome. So it is with material. Everything has its atomic number, number of atoms indicating how slowly it is going to vibrate, or how fast it is going to vibrate. So all we do in pendulum work is to tune in to some atomic vibrations, and, if we know how, we can tell which one it is and where it is.

When we are dealing with radio waves, we have an aerial system which absorbs or attracts or intercepts (call it what you like) the waves coming through the atmosphere. In addition there is a ground wire, which makes contact with the ground wave – because you must have two – positive and negative – in everything. You can take the ground wave as negative and the air wave as positive. So in the matter of pendulums the human body collects the air wave, acting as the antenna or aerial, and the feet in contact with the ground act as the earth connection, or ground. And for correct pendulum work it is necessary to keep the balls of the feet on the ground, unless one uses another method of tapping the earth current.

Of course, using a pendulum is simplicity itself. It is even simpler than simplicity if we know why a thing works. That's why you are getting this long collection of words which might at first strike you as rigmarole; it's not. <u>Until you know what you are doing you can't tell when you are doing it!</u>

Pendulums really work! Many Japanese tell the sex of unborn babies by the use of a pendulum. They use a gold ring suspended on a piece of string or thread, and it is held above the stomach of the pregnant woman. The direction or type of movement indicates the sex of the child yet to be born. Incidentally, many Chinese and Japanese use a pendulum for sexing chicken eggs!

A radio set uses electric current for reproducing sound which was broadcast from some distant station. Television sets use current also for reproducing a rough simulacrum of the picture transmitted from a distant station. So in the same way if we are going to dowse or use a pendulum or anything else, we have first of all to have a source of current, and the best source of current we can use is the human body. After all, our brains are really storage batteries, telephone exchanges, and all that sort of thing, but the main thing is, it is a source of electric current – sufficient for all our needs and sufficient to enable us to 'detect' impulses, and thereby cause a pendulum to twitch, swirl, gyrate, or oscillate, or all the other queer things which a pendulum does. So, to work a pendulum, we must have a human body, an alive human body at that. You cannot tie a pendulum to a hook and expect it to work, because there would be no source of current.

Nor would it be of much use if we could tie our pendulum to a hook and supply it with current because the current has to be in pulses varying according to the type of action desired. Just as in radio, we have high notes, low notes, loud notes, and soft notes, so with a pendulum we must have the necessary current variation to do "the necessary."

Who is going to vary the current? Well, the Overself, of course. That is the brightest citizen we have around us, you know. After all, you who read this are just one tenth conscious, so, knowing yourself, just think how brilliant you would be if you could call in the other nine tenths of consciousness. You can certainly enlist its aid, the aid of the subconscious. The subconscious is brilliant; it knows everything that you have ever known, can do everything that you could ever do, and can remember every single incident since long before you were born. So if you could touch your subconscious, you would get to know a very considerable amount of things, wouldn't you? You can reach out and touch your subconscious, with practice and with confidence.

The subconscious can also contact other subconscious minds. There are truthfully no limits to the powers of the subconscious mind and when the subconscious mind is allied to other subconscious minds, then indeed results may be achieved.

We cannot just ring up a telephone number and ask to speak to our subconscious, because we have to look upon that Mind as being something like a very absent minded professor who is constantly sorting knowledge, storing knowledge, and acquiring knowledge. He is so busy that he can't bother with other people. If you pester him enough in the most polite way, then he may answer your summons.

My Visit To Agharta

So first of all you have to become familiar with your subconscious. You see, the whole thing is that the subconscious is the greater part of you, the much greater part of you, and I suggest that you give your subconscious a name. Call him or her whatever you like so long as it is a name agreeable to you. The whole point is that you must have some definite name, which you link inseparably with your subconscious. So when you want to get in touch with your subconscious, you could say for example, "George, George, I want your help very much, I want you to work with me, I want you to (here you specify what you want), and remember, George, that really we are all one and what you do for me you are also doing for yourself." You need to repeat that slowly and carefully, and with very great thought. Repeat it three times!!

The first time George will probably shrug his mental shoulders and say, "Oh that pestiferous fellow, bothering me again when I've got so much work to do," and he will turn back to his work. Next time you repeat it he will pay more attention because he is being bothered, but still he won't take any action. But if you repeat it a third time, "George" or "Peter" or "Sally" or whoever it is, will get the idea that you are going to keep on until you get some action, so he will give a metaphorical sigh and help.

This is not fantasy, it's fact. I claim to know quite a lot about it, because for more years than I care to remember, I have done just this. My own subconscious is not called "George," by the way, but a name which I do not reveal to anyone else, just as you should not reveal to anyone else the name of your subconscious. Never laugh or joke about it because this is deadly serious. You are only one/tenth of a person, your subconscious is nine/tenths, so you have to show respect, you have to show affection, you have to show that you can be trusted because if you do not gain the cooperation of your subconscious then you won't do any of the things that I write about. But if you practice what you are reading, you can do the whole lot. So make friends with your subconscious. Give him or her a name, and be sure that you keep that name very, very private indeed.

You can talk to your subconscious. It is better if you talk slowly and repeat things. Imagine that you are telephoning someone on the other side of the world and the telephone line is a bit poor, you have to repeat yourself, you have quite a difficult time making yourself understood. Your listener at the other end of the telephone line is not an idiot for having difficulty in understanding your message, but general communications are bad, and if you overcome the difficulties of communications – you can then find that you have a very intelligent conversationalist, one who is far more intelligent than you are!

When you are using the pendulum you have to keep your feet flat on the ground so that the balls of your feet are in contact with the floor, and then you have to say something like, "Subconscious (or the name you have chosen), I want to know what I must do to get success at such - and - such a thing. if you are going to make the pendulum work, will you make it swing backwards and forwards to indicate YES, and from side to side to indicate NO – just as a human does when he nods for YES and shakes his head for NO."

You have to get over a message like that about three times, you have to explain very slowly, very dearly, and very carefully indeed what you want your subconscious to do and what you expect of the test – because if you don't know what you want, then how can the subconscious give you any information? The subconscious won't know either. If you don't know what you want, you don't know when you've found it!

THE DOWSING PENDULUM

The dowsing pendulum should be a ball possibly an inch or an inch and a quarter in diameter (25-30mm). If you can get a very good wooden pendulum so much the better, or you may be able to obtain a "neutral metal" one. A small fishing weight, or even a ring will work nicely. But for the moment any pendulum will do as long as it is about an inch or an inch and a quarter in diameter.

You should get a piece of thread such as boot makers use for stitching on soles. I believe it's called cobblers' thread. You will need about five feet of it. Tie one end to your pendulum which should have a little eyelet on the top for that purpose, and tie the other end to a rod or even to an empty cotton reel. Then wind all the thread on to the cotton reel so that when you hold the small cotton reel in the palm of your hand the thread holding the pendulum is between the finger and thumb of your right hand, your right hand if you write with that one, but if you use your left hand instead, then, of course, the pendulum will be in the left hand. But first we have to sensitize, or tune, our pendulum for the particular type of material we wish to locate.

My Visit To Agharta

Supposing we are going to look for a gold mine; first of all you get a little piece of sticky tape, about an inch long is sufficient, and then you put just a very small piece of gold (scraped from inside a ring, for instance) on to the sticky tape and then just lightly push it on to the pendulum. Then your pendulum has a piece of gold which will sensitize it to that metal, and when I say "scrape" – I mean that even if you get a grain, that will be adequate.

When you have that, put your ring, or another piece of gold, between your feet as you stand up. Stand with this gold, such as a gold ring or a gold watch, between your feet and slowly unwind the thread so that your pendulum lowers to perhaps a foot and a half (45cm) from your fingers. At this point the pendulum should swing in a circular direction, that is, making a complete circle. If it does not do so, lower the thread a little or pull it up a little, the point being, you have to ascertain the length of thread at which the pendulum swings most freely for gold.

When you have determined that – it may be eighteen or twenty or twenty two inches or similar – you make a knot in the thread and you write down the exact length, such as "Knot One - Gold," and then you pull off your gold specimen with the tape and pick up your watch or ring, and put a silver article on the floor; it may be a coin or a piece of silver you have pinched from somebody else, but it must be silver. You also put a very fine scraping of silver on another piece of tape and put that on to your pendulum. Then you try again to find what is the correct length for silver. When you have done that you make another note such as "Knot Two - Silver."

You can go on doing it for different metals, and not only different metals but different substances. If you make a proper table, then you should have great fun prospecting. Generally you will find that in terms of length, the first thing to respond (at about twelve inches in length) is stonework. A bit longer thread, and you will get glass or chinaware. Longer still and you will get vegetable stuff.

Go on increasing the length and you will get silver and lead, and then a bit further on you will find water. Longer still, you will find gold. Still longer, copper and brass. And the longest will be iron, and iron will be roughly just under thirty inches (76cm). So if you want to know what is beneath you, you just stand there and first of all think of whatever metal you are looking for. You adjust the length of your thread to the appropriate distance, and you very slowly walk forward.

My Visit To Agharta

Again – it is emphasized and reemphasized that you must tell George precisely what you are doing. You have to tell him that you want to prospect for gold, iron, silver, or whatever it is, and when he senses the radiations will he please swing the pendulum. At all times you must definitely keep thinking very strongly of that which you hope to find; otherwise, if you change over and think of something else, you will confuse the issue and nothing will be found.

Apropos of this – let me say that if you are looking for antique porcelain, for instance, and you suddenly think of women, then you will get the reaction for gold because the length of thread for gold and for women is precisely the same, and if a woman thinks about men she will get the reaction as if there was a diamond under the ground! That, of course, means that you will be completely misled. It would never do if you got the reaction for a diamond so you grabbed a shovel and pick and dug, but found instead a dead man. It could happen!

Now, it is advisable to use a shorter cord pendulum for everyday indoor use. After all, you don't want three, four, or five feet of thread getting tangled up every day. So when you are indoors use a separate pendulum. The pendulums which can be obtained commercially already have a thread or a chain attached to them, and frequently the chain is possibly six inches long, although the exact length varies, but that is of no concern.

Suppose you want to find something – suppose you want to find out if a person is living in a certain area; then you sit down at a desk or, table, but it must be an ordinary desk or table with no drawers or anything beneath because if you have anything beneath in, for example, a drawer, then the pendulum will be influenced by whatever is in the drawer.

You may have a kitchen knife in the drawer. You may have a gold ring or something like that, and the pendulum, no matter how hard you think of your subject, will be influenced by the "wrong" thing. So sit at a plain table and have within arm's reach some sheets of ordinary plain white paper. Then you tell your pendulum, or rather you tell George exactly what you want. You say, for example, "Look, George, I want to find if Maria Bugsbottom lives in this area. If she does, will you please nod by giving the pendulum a backwards and forwards movement, and if she does not will you please shake the pendulum from side to side."

129

My Visit To Agharta

Then on the right hand side of the table you have your piece of white paper, and on the top which is far away from you – you put YES, and on the bottom which is close to you put YES. On the far left side of the paper you put NO and on the far right side you put NO, and in the center you put a little X to show that is the spot over which you are going to hold the pendulum. The pendulum, by the way, should be held about two inches above that X.

Sit comfortably. It doesn't matter if you have your shoes on or your shoes off, but you must have your feet on the floor, not on the bars of a chair – have them flat on the floor so that the balls of your feet are in contact with the floor. Then you get a map of the area desired and spread it to your left so that you have a white sheet of paper to the right and your map on the left. First you gently take the, pendulum all over the area of the map, saying, "Look, George, this is the area of my map. Is Maria Bugsbottom anywhere within this area?"

The pendulum being taken over the map about two inches above the surface. When you have covered the whole area, you say, "George – I am now going to start this investigation. Will you help me, George? Will you indicate YES or NO as the case may be?"

Then (if you are right handed), put your right elbow comfortably on the table and suspend your pendulum by its thread or chain, hold the thread or chain between your thumb and forefinger (the finger with which you point). See that the pendulum is about two inches above the X. Special note here – if you are left handed everything will have to be reversed, but for the right handed – well, go by the instructions conveyed above.

Having got ready, and making sure that you are not likely to be disturbed, tell George that you are now ready to start work. Look at the map and put your left forefinger along the road on the map where you think Maria Bugsbottom may be living. Give an occasional glance at the pendulum. It may swing idly without any apparent sense, but if you get to where you believe your friend or enemy is living, then the pendulum will definitely indicate yea or nay.

It is a good idea to use a small scale map first so that you can cover the biggest area, but when you get some sort of indication as if George was saying, "Gee! I need to get closer than this," then you need to get a large scale map.

My Visit To Agharta

After each test you definitely must replace your sheet of white paper by another, you can use it for writing on; write letters on it or anything else, but only one sheet of white paper to one reading because you have impregnated that sheet with the impressions of whatever you are trying to find out so that if you try to repeat a reading, then the second reading will be influenced by the first and, well, that's all there is to it.

But no, perhaps that's not all there is to it after all – because you've got to really frame your questions properly. George, you see, is a single minded individual who can't take a joke and is extremely and exceptionally literal. So it's no good you saying, "George, can you tell me if Maria Bugsbottom lives there?" If you ask a question like that the answer will be YES, because George can tell you if Maria Bngsbottom lives there, he can. And that is what you are asking. You are asking with a question in that form if the pendulum can tell you. You are not asking if she is actually living there at the moment. So whatever question you ask must be framed in such a way that George is not in a state of confusion.

The biggest difficulty about the whole affair is framing the questions, so that they are fool proof, so that there are no double meanings to them. In any question if you say, "Can you tell me?," then the answer will be YES or NO to the question of 'Can you tell me?' The other part of the question, "if Maria Bugsbottom lives there?" will be unanswered because the first question will have swamped George's interest and he won't answer.

So until you are more practiced at this how about writing out your questions first and looking at your words to see if there is any way at all in which the question can be regarded as ambiguous or as having a double meaning or is unclear. Let me repeat in big, bold, black capitals – YOU MUST BE SURE OF WHAT YOU ARE ASKING BEFORE YOU CAN POSE THE QUESTION.

Of course, when you have some practice it's quite easy to trace missing people. You have to have a small scale and a large scale map of the area in which the person is supposed to be missing. Then you have to be able to form some sort of mental picture of the person who is missing. Is it a big boy or a small girl? Is he or she ginger, blonde, or black haired? What do you know about the person? You have to brief yourself as fully as possible, because, again, unless you know what you are seeking, then you don't know when you've found it.

131

My Visit To Agharta

It may happen at times when, for example, you are confined to bed, that you cannot stick your feet plunk on the ground. That is my trouble, so I have a metal wand about two and a half feet long, and I hold that in my left hand just like an antennae system to a portable radio, in fact that's what it is; it is an antenna rod from a portable radio. I pick up the wave from that in precisely the same manner as a more mobile person would with two flat feet.

When I am picking up impressions from a map or a letter, then I use a little propelling pencil, a metal one, and I touch the letter or the map and then the old pendulum starts to wobble and gives me an answer.

Never, never, never let anyone else touch your pendulum. It's got to be saturated with your own impressions. You should have several pendulums, one of wood, one of neutral metal, and you may want a crystal one, or you may want a plastic one, you may even have one which is hollow so you can put a specimen inside instead of sticking it up with tape. But you will find one pendulum is more responsive than all the others for personal things, and you can make it even more responsive by carrying it on your person, getting saturated with your own impressions. If you do that and never let another person use it or even touch it, then you will find you have something as potent and as useful as radar is to aircraft on a foggy night.

The pendulum cannot be wrong. George cannot be wrong. You can. You can go wrong with the form your questions take and your interpretations of the answers. Now, with computers one has to use a special language, otherwise the computer can not make sense of what one is trying to get at, so pretend that your pendulum is a computer and frame your questions in such a dear one way form that no possibility of error can occur because the pendulum can only indicate YES or NO.

It can indicate uncertainty by doing a figure of eight. It can also indicate what sex a thing or a person is because most times for a man it can rotate in a right hand circle, clockwise that is, but for a woman it will rotate in a left and, anticlockwise, circle. But if the man is very feminine then the poor old pendulum may go the wrong way, but it's not actually the wrong way, it is just indicating that the man isn't, he's more female and just has the necessary attachments, as one would say in the best circles, which would enable him to pass physiologically as a male specimen. All his thoughts may be female, so in that way the pendulum is far better as a judge than the best doctors!

132

My Visit To Agharta

Oh yes, I must be sure to tell you this; make sure your hands are clean before using the pendulum, otherwise, if, for instance, you have been gardening or stubbing out a cigarette butt in some poor plant's plant pot home, then you will get a reading for the soil content of the pores of your fingers. So be sure that your fingers and hands are clean. Be sure that your table is clean. It's no good, for instance, turning around and finding that a big fat cat is sitting on a sheet of white paper, and if it is then you have to use a different sheet of white paper!

With a pendulum and practice you can know how to dowse for minerals from a map. You go along looking for gold if you like, by having a little particle of gold attached to the pendulum. Then you let your finger go along the map to the location where you think there may be gold, and you think strongly of gold to the exclusion of all else. Or, if you are looking for silver, think strongly of silver to the exclusion of all else. All these things are very, very simple; until you get used to them you will be sure they are utterly impossible – they are not for you. But they are. It is only practice that makes a pilot able to take off in his aircraft and bring it down in one piece. It is only practice and faith in yourself, that will enable you to go to your table, produce a map and a pendulum, and say, "There – there is water, floods of it," and then go to the actual site and find upon digging that the water is at a certain depth.

You can get a good idea of the depth of a thing by the strength of the oscillation or movement of the pendulum. Practice will soon teach you how to shorten or lengthen the chain or string, and how to gauge depth. But remember again that you must very definitely and strongly concentrate on that which you want to find or know.

You can also find out a lot about a person by using a pendulum over the signature on the letter. It is quite a useful exercise. But, remember, you must be sure of what you want to know, you must be sure of what you are asking, because if you are asking a thing in two parts, then George is sure to answer the wrong one! And be very certain that you tell your subconscious – George or whatever you call him or her – precisely what you are trying to find out and what you expect the pendulum to do to indicate the information you desire.

To hold the pendulum properly, one rests one's elbow on the table, as already stated, and it should be the right elbow for a right handed person and the left elbow for a left handed person. Then you bend your arm so that your hand is at such a height from the table that your pendulum, which is suspended at the end of its chain or string, rests about two inches (5cm) above the surface of the table. You actually hold the chain, string, cord, or whatever it is between your thumb and forefinger, and if you want to shorten the chain an inch or so in order to get a better swing – well, do so.

Always adjust the length of the chain or thread between your finger and thumb so as to get the best swing or indication. Now, that should be clear enough – you just hold your forearm at such an angle that you are comfortable. You must be comfortable or you will not be able to do pendulum work. Similarly, if you have just had a heavy meal you will not be able to do pendulum work, or if you have something bothering you greatly unconnected with this pendulum, it will distract your attention. You must be in a fairly quiet state of mind, and you must be willing to work with the subconscious.

You want your pendulum to tell you where such - and - such a thing is, so it might be a lump of gold and in that case you will tune your pendulum for a lump of gold. Then you will visualize yourself holding the pendulum by its cord and the swing indicating gold. You will pick up a map and you will try to locate gold through the use of the map. If you convey the idea with complete clarity and point out the advantages to the subconscious, then you will be able to detect gold if there is any there.

THE OVERSELF AND THE SUBCONSCIOUS

Now, I am also told, 'You've got me all confused; you say the Overself is going to vary the current – well, what is the connection between the Overself and the subconscious?'

Let us try to get this clear for ever and a day or a bit longer; there is you who is just one/tenth conscious. You are bottom man on the ladder, or you might even be bottom woman on the ladder. Above you – you have your subconscious, and your subconscious is like the operator who controls the switchboard, etc., which is your brain. The subconscious is in touch with you through your brain – through your joint brain would perhaps be a better term – and the subconscious is also in touch with your Overself. So it's like you, the ordinary poor worker, who cannot get a word with the manager, you have to go through the shop steward or the foreman first. So you sort of hang around, try to make yourself obtrusive in the hope that the shop steward or the one above you will notice you, and wondering why you are not at work will come and see what it's all about. Then you have to get your point of view over to the shop steward or foreman, and persuade him to take up your case with the manager or whoever is above him. This is similar to conditions with the Overself and you. Before you can get through to your Overself – you have to enlist the aid of your subconscious, and once you can convince your subconscious that it's really necessary for your joint good, then the subconscious will contact the Overself and the pendulum will be varied according to the indications which you are perceiving.

Incidentally, if you can get through to your Overself by way of the subconscious you can cure a lot of illnesses which you may have. The Overself is like the president of a company and he doesn't always know what minor ailments affect the lower departments. He knows it in times when conditions are very, very serious, but often he is in complete ignorance of some grievance, which the lower order of workers have. But if you can get your shop steward to take up the matter with the Overself, or president, or general manager, then a grievance can be settled before it becomes serious. So if you have a persistent ache here, there, or somewhere else, then keep on at George or Georgina, say clearly what the trouble is, what is this pain, what does it feel like, why do you have it, and will the subconscious please see that you are cured. The Overself is the unapproachable. The subconscious is the link between you, the one/tenth conscious, and the Overself which is all conscious.

Oh sure, of course the pendulum can help you pick the winner of a race if you phrase your question sensibly, but look at this. "Can you tell me who will win the two-thirty race?" Now what sort of a question is that? Look at it seriously and you will see that you are asking your subconscious to tell you this; can you, subconscious, tell me who will win the race? The answer, of course, would be YES, and if you get a yes in answer to your question, you would think you were being fooled, wouldn't you? You can't do it that way at all. You must be clear and precise with your questions.

Now, in this case if you want to know who is going to win a certain race, you will have to get a list of horses, the horses who are going to run in that specific race, and you will have to think definitely, "Will this horse win?" And you will have to bring the pencil in your left hand slowly down to each name in turn, leaving it there about thirty seconds and thinking about that horse for about thirty seconds, asking if this horse will win the race. If the answer is NO, then go on to the next horse until you've got to the one that is going to win. You can do it with practice.

It's not very moral, you know, because betting and gambling are bad things, but anyway that is your own responsibility. I am just trying to make absolutely clear to you that you won't get any satisfactory result unless you quite definitely phrase your question in such a manner that there is only one question involved, a question which can be answered by a plain YES or a plain NO. I suggest you read that bit again because otherwise you are going to be really cross when you get a mixed up answer which really will be a mixed up questioner.

Practice is the key to everything. You cannot be a great pianist unless you practice. The more important the pianist the more he or she practices – hours a day of those silly scales going "bonk, bonk, bonk." It is the same with a pendulum; you have to practice and practice and practice, so you can do it by instinct, and you can practice with people's letters, with metals and all the rest of it, and that's the way you will make a success – practice.

Oh yes! There is one other little point which I should mention. I will mention it but, naturally, I would expect that the ordinary rules of politeness would apply; it is very, very important indeed that after you have used your pendulum you clasp it in your two hands to your forehead and then you solemnly thank George or Georgina for assisting you in this reading. "Thank you" three times, do not forget that, because if you do not thank "him" or "her" according to the elementary rules of politeness, you may not get a response in two or three times hence, and remember, your thanks must be repeated thrice just as your requests have been.

I am told that I do not make it clear how some poor wretch should stand when he or she is tuning the pendulum with a lump of gold or a crummy bit of silver between the feet. Okay, here it is, you get your gold, silver, tin, lead, or copper and you put it on the ground between your feet. Then you stand upright with your spine straight and your left arm down by your side. Then you elevate your right hand so that your forearm is parallel to the ground and you see if that is a convenient method of doing it – because if you brace your right elbow against your side, you will not get undesired wobbles or squiggles in your pendulum but only what George dictates. But the main thing, of course, is – hold your arm at any distance convenient for you and convenient for the pendulum. And that's all there is to it!

DEVELOPING YOUR LATENT OCCULT ABILITIES

Some people have asked me why they have problems doing some of the things that I have described in my books – like astral travel or using the pendulum. If you find difficulty in doing something, then are you sure, really sure, that you want to do it? Are you sure that there is not some bar imposed, let us say, by difficulties in a past life?

Supposing a person – oh, not you, of course! – had been a witch in a past life. Supposing you had been burned at the stake or bumped off in some equally interesting way, then if you came back to this life with more or less of an interest in occultism you might have some ingrained fear that if you started again you would end up at the stake or at the end of a rope, and so your subconscious would clap the brakes on and you would make no progress.

The only way one can proceed if one finds real difficulty in settling down to occult work is:

❑ **Meditate on the problem. Do you really, sincerely desire to astral travel or to do clairvoyance or read the cards or do anything in that field?**

❑ **If you do, if you can say YES, then ask yourself why you want to do it. You must clear up all these problems first.**

The next thing to ask yourself is, do you fear that you will be out of the body and will not be able to get back, are you afraid that some strange entities will attack you if you get out of the body? If so, remember that no harm whatsoever, no harm of any sort can happen to you if you are not afraid.

If you are sure that you really want to do occult work, then the best thing is to devote a certain time each day, even half an hour of an evening, to thinking about it. And the best way is to imagine as strongly as possible that you are doing what you want to do, because when you can get over to your subconscious that you want to get out into the astral he will, metaphorically, unlock the gate and set you free. Think of the sub-conscious as a sort of idiot, a high-grade idiot, if you like, who obeys orders quite literally so that if at some time in the past you have said, "Gee! For Pete's sake don't let me get out of the body!" then the subconscious will obey that injunction until you can overpower its one-track mind and replace the obsolete order by another.

But remember that if you think you are not making progress, you definitely are so long as you are aware of things. And my strong advice to you is that if you are experiencing obstacles or difficulties, then just do not bother, wait until things settle themselves.

When I was studying morse code many years ago I was warned about "the hump." Well, this mysterious hump bothered me until I reached a speed of twenty-three words a minute, and no matter how much I tried, I could not get over that "hump." It proved to be a mountain in the way of my progress towards a faster, morse code sending and receiving speed.

One day I uttered some really naughty words with fervour. I said, in effect, "Oh well, if I can't go any faster I just can't." Later in the day I sat down at the old morse key again and found that I could go much faster, in fact I could do nearly thirty words a minute. I had got over the hump. I had been trying too hard, and if you are having troubles, probably you are trying too hard as well. If you are meeting obstacles don't go on like a bulldozer, take it easy, think about things, and you will find that the path of least resistance has enabled you to get over the hump, and you will be surprised at the result.

WHAT IS THE MEANING OF IT ALL?

The Overself cannot of itself experience desire, suffering, pleasure, etc., as we know it on Earth, and so it is necessary for the Overself to have some other method of gaining knowledge. People upon Earth are just extensions of the Overself, which can gain knowledge. For example, suppose you have a bag and you cannot get inside the bag and you cannot see inside the bag. If you can get it open enough to get your hand in, your hand, which is an extension of your other senses, can feel around inside the bag and can tell the brain what there is inside. In much the same way the Overself gains information through the extensions called human beings.

My Visit To Agharta

When the Overself has sufficient knowledge, when the Overself is so advanced that no more knowledge on the Earth cycle is desired, then it calls home all the puppets which are humans, and they all merge again into the Overself, they become united in 'Oneness'; that is the ultimate form of existence, because although it seems to be just one entity, each part of the entity lives in rapport with the other part.

You have heard of twin souls – well, on the Earth plane – it is impossible for twin souls to get together, but when they return to the Overself twin souls are reunited to form a perfect whole, and they live in a state of very great bliss until it occurs to the Overself that perhaps there is yet a higher form of knowledge which could be investigated. And then the Overself sends out puppets, not on the Earth plane, but on some super plane, and the whole cycle is repeated. The puppets gather in the knowledge throughout a period, which to us is eons of time. Again, when sufficient experience or knowledge has been garnered, the Overself calls in the puppets, twin souls are again united in an even greater state of bliss.

Because of this, karma is of vital importance to all of us, and in my books you have an opportunity of knowing what karma is all about. It means, in brief, that if you do something wrong you pay for it. If you do something good, something pays you. As I have said before, it is like a bank account. You are like a storekeeper who has good and bad, on the shelves. If you sell something that is good then you get paid by good, if you sell something that is bad you get paid by having an overdraft.

Now get this quite clear; whatever you do does not necessarily and automatically have an effect on any other person or creature. It depends entirely upon the circumstances. If, for example, you take a dagger and stick it into a person, then, of course doing a good deed, are you? In that case then you do not have karma against you. But if you do something which has an effect, a bad effect upon a person you have never heard of, an effect which you certainly did not anticipate, then you do not have to come back and pay off that person.

Everything that we do in this life will have an effect not only in your next life, but also in the astral worlds. There are many who pass beyond the Earth to the next life with the firm, absolutely unbreakable conviction that their own particular religion is the only one which can exist. These poor wretches are in much the same position because the helpers on the Other Side know quite well that they cannot help the newcomer if their mere appearance shatters a lifelong belief, so let us suppose a person is a very strong Catholic believing in angels and devils and all the rest of that pantomime. Then, when they get to the Other Side they do indeed see the Pearly Gates, they see an old fellow with a beard and a whacking great ledger in which they think all the sins are being recorded.

Everything is done to put on the sort of show that the good, ignorant Catholic wants to see. He sees angels with flapping wings, he sees people sitting on clouds playing harps, and for a time he is quite satisfied thinking he has reached Heaven. But gradually it dawns on him that all this doesn't ring true, the people do not fly in the right rhythm for beating wings, etc., etc. Gradually it dawns on the newcomer that all this is a stage show and he begins to wonder what is behind it all, what is behind the drapes and the set piece, what are things really like, and just as soon as he begins to think that way he begins to see "cracks" in the facade of the Heavenly Crowd. Soon there comes a time when he cannot stick the pantomime any longer and he cries out for enlightenment.

Quickly the angels with their flapping wings fade away, quickly the harpists sitting in their nightshirts on a cloud beat it, quickly highly trained, highly experienced helpers show the newly awakened newcomer the reality instead of the illusion, and the reality is far greater than the illusion ever could be. It is a sad fact that so many people see a few pictures in the Bible and they take them for gospel.

No matter what religion it is, if there are adherents who believe unswervingly in the legends and, let us say, fantasies, of that religion, then that is what they see when they leave the Earth and enter the astral plane.

When the newcomer can realize the nature of the world he is in, then he can proceed further. He goes to the Hall of Memories and there, alone; he enters a room and he sees the whole of his life, everything he has done, everything he has tried to do, and everything he wanted to do. He sees everything that happened to him, and everything that he thought while upon the Earth, and he, and he alone, can make a judgement of whether his life was a success or a failure.

He, and he alone, can decide whether he will "go back to college" and start the Course all over again in the hope of passing successfully next time. There is no mother or father or best friend to stand by and take the blame for anything that he has done wrongly, he is there alone, entirely alone, more alone than he has been since he stood in that place before, last time. And he judges himself. No devils, no Satan waiting with twitching tail and fiery breath, nobody is going to jab pitchforks into him, and as for all the flames, well, they don't even use such things for central heating!

There are more and more people coming to the Earth, more and more people being born to the Earth, and many inquirers wonder why that should be so. The answer is Earth is just one speck of dust amid billions of specks of dust, and when people ask me why the population of the Earth is increasing I tell them the truth, which is that people are coming to Earth from other more nebulous planes of existence.

Perhaps a person comes from a two dimensional world and comes to Earth as his first experience in a three dimensional world, so he starts his round of existence to the three dimensional world which we call Earth. And all the time there are more and more people coming as Earth becomes more and more of a qualified school of hardship. That is the purpose of Earth, you know, to teach one hardship and how to endure it and how to overcome it. People do not come to Earth to have a very enjoyable time, they come to learn so that all the information they learn can be passed on to the Overself.

After this world there is the astral plane, and from the astral plane, in the fullness of time, one is born upwards to different planes of existence until at last the fully evolved entity merges with the Overself. That is how the Overself grows. If, having grown quite a lot, the Overself decides that there is much more to learn, then fresh souls are put down on some world and the whole process of cycles of life is started all over again; and each time when the souls have completed their cycles they return purified to the Overself, which, again, grows through it.

I hope that I have answered some of your questions. Of course there are many questions that can never really be answered in this lifetime. That is the great mystery of our existence. Some things are just not meant for us to know while on Earth. But take comfort in the fact that despite the problems that exist in our world – everything is really all right. With love and forgiveness toward each other, we can make this world, this universe, a better place. This I believe is the ultimate reflection of the Creator: love and forgiveness really does conquer all.

The Lobsang Rampa Photo Album

"Living With the Lama"

A man and his cat, here is a photo of Lobsang and his cat Miss Cleopatra.

Lobsang relaxes at home.

PRODUCTS INSPIRED BY RAMPA

Rampa did not believe in a lot of "bells and whistles." But he did talk of using a meditation stone and was a big believer in alternative methods of healing. Thus we are offering the following RAMPA INSPIRED PRODUCTS to use for your spiritual and physical well being. Send all orders to Inner Light, Box 753, New Brunswick, NJ 08903 (732 602-3407). Add $5 for S/H. in U.S. or $10 foreign. NJ residents add sales tax. Enjoy and prosper!

Kwan Yin Carvings

One of the most widely honored aspects of the Goddess is Kwan Yin. Known as the Bodhisattva of Compassion, Kwan Yin is the Buddhist representa-tion of the same type of energy worshiped else-where as Mary, and by other names as well. Kwan Yin is believed to be a protector, a helper to those with legal problems, a healer to the sick. She is the kind and nurturing aspect of the feminine power.

We recently found a Chinese source for incredi-bly detailed carved images of Kwan Yin in cabo-chons of clear Quartz crystal. They are painstakingly carved into the back of the Quartz stone, so that from the front Kwan Yin appears as an image of sculpted beauty in frosted white, floating in the unblemished clarity of the clear Quartz.

Radha tells us, "As I have said before, images of the Divine can evoke their presence within us. That is what all symbols are good for. Wearing, carrying or meditating with these Kwan Yin talismans can bring Her energy more fully into one's life. And the clear Quartz into which her image is carved is an amplifier of the beneficial energies which are mag-netized by the image and the intent of the user. These lovely stones are ideal for wear as pendants, or as pocket stones, I would even recommend them for crystal healing body layouts. The combination of the Quartz and the Divine image is one I would personally choose for spiritual self-healing work."